Plain legal language for a new democracy

I herewith in
solemn submission
aforesaid and aforementioned
and mutatis mutandis
find applicant hereinunder
case in casu notwithstanding
undertaken by aforesaid
henceforth null and
void and of no force
and effect

# Plain legal language for a new democracy

**Frans Viljoen** and **Annelize Nienaber** (eds)

Protea Book House
Pretoria
2001

Plain legal language for a new democracy

First edition, 2001
Protea Book House
PO Box 35110, Menlopark, 0102
protea@intekom.co.za


Typography & design by HOND BK
Cover design by HOND BK
Reproduction by PrePress Images, Pretoria
Printed & bound ABC Press

ISBN 1–919825–53–3


© All rights reserved.
No part of this book may be reproduced in any form,
without prior permission in writing from the publisher.

# Plain legal language for a new democracy

**A  Introduction** — *page 9*

**B  What is plain language?** — *page 17*
   1  Plain language communication: Approaches and challenges *(Derrick Fine)*

**C  What's happening? Plain language in the international context** — *page 27*
   1  Introduction *(Frans Viljoen & Annelize Nienaber)*
   2  Plain language in Australia: An overview *(Annelize Nienaber)*
   3  Current developments in the UK *(Mark Adler)*
   4  The plain language experience in the USA *(Frans Viljoen)*

**D  Plain legal language in South Africa** — *page 53*
   1  Plain language, the law and the right to information *(Dullah Omar)*
   2  Plain language in the drafting of the 1996 Constitution *(Johann van der Westhuizen)*
   3  Some concise guidelines to the process of drafting the new Labour Relations Act in plain language *(Amanda Armstrong)*
   4  Plain language in the current practice of drafting *(Enver Daniels)*
   5  A practitioner's perspective: Leases in plain language *(Chris Leppan)*
   6  Plain language in a multilingual society *(Mariëtta Alberts)*

**E  Research on plain legal language in South Africa** — *page 119*
   1  Plain language in South Africa: Report on an empirical research project *(Frans Viljoen & Annelize Nienaber)*

**F  Conclusion** — *page 155*
   1  Conclusion *(Frans Viljoen & Annelize Nienaber)*
   2  Launch of Clarity in South Africa *(Mark Adler)*

**G  Plain language sources** — *page 161*
   1  General sources
   2  Sources with a South African focus
   3  General webpages
   4  Webpages of South African interest

**H  Contributors** — *page 171*

# A
# Introduction

A.1 Introduction — page 9

## A.1
# Introduction

**Frans Viljoen**
*Faculty of Law, University of Pretoria*

**Annelize Nienaber**
*Faculty of Law, University of Pretoria*

---
1 Plain language in South Africa ... *page 9*
2 Conference and workshop ... *page 12*
3 Overview of this book ... *page 12*
4 Acknowledgement of financial support ... *page 15*

---

## 1   Plain language in South Africa

### 1.1   Historical background

Plain legal language was not a priority of governments in South Africa before 1994. As the 20$^{th}$ century progressed, the South African legal system suffered a crisis of legitimacy. The discriminatory nature of racially-based apartheid laws lay at the heart of the crisis. In South Africa, racial difference usually indicates language difference. The issue of language became overtly politicised after the 1976 Soweto uprising. People's access to the law was not limited only because Afrikaans and English were used exclusively, but because legal language was complicated and inaccessible. In a culture where basic rights were denied, informing people of their rights was not a concern. In short, there was no room, no need, for plain legal language.

Obscurity and inaccessibility extended to relatively mundane affairs, as reflected in the Water Act (54 of 1956). Section 9B (1) (a) of the Act reads as follows:

**Control of impounding or abstraction of public water in excess of a certain quantity**

Notwithstanding anything to the contrary contained in this Act or any other law but subject to the provisions of a notice under subsection (1C), no person shall construct, alter or enlarge any water work on one or more pieces of land which on the date of commencement of the Water Amendment Act, 1975, were registered in the deeds registry as a separate piece or separate pieces of land or where such piece of land has been or will be subdivided subsequent to the said date, on one or more of those subdivisions and any other piece of land, if more than 250 000 cubic meters of public water are or, after completion of such construction, alteration or enlargement, will be capable of being impounded or stored or more than 110 litres of water per second are or, after such completion, will be capable of being abstracted or diverted from a public stream, in or by means of that water work, or that water work and any other water work or water works on the piece of land concerned or any of the subdivisions concerned, except under the authority of a permit issued by the Minister, and on such conditions as may be specified in that permit, which may include conditions relating to the operation of any of the water works concerned.

A well-known jurist, JC de Wet, scathingly criticised this Act:
> Is it technically impossible to draft a proper water statute in less than 50 000 words? There must be something drastically wrong if a statute that regulates water law requires half the number of words of the whole Greek Civil Code.
> (Our translation, original Afrikaans quoted in Kahn, E *Law, Life & laughter* (1991) 47)

## 1.2 Time for change

After 1990, the transition to democracy made plain legal language possible. Politicians started formulating the features of a future democratic society. Understandably, substance prevailed over style in the Interim Constitution of 1993. However, after the adoption of the Interim Constitution it became clear to a significant number of people that its complex and legalistic wording could dilute its promise of equality.

A group of international plain language experts (including Christopher Balmford (Australia), Joseph Kimble (Thomas Cooley Law School, USA), Phil Knight (Canada), Shadrack Gutto (South

Africa) and two representatives from the Plain English Campaign (UK)) visited South Africa in order to advise the Constitutional Assembly on drafting the Final Constitution. The Ministry of Justice organised a conference on the topic in March 1995, with the aim of giving importance to plain language concerns.

The impact of the international team of plain language experts is illustrated by a comparison of the Interim and Final Constitutions. They also clearly left their mark on post-1994 legislation such as the Labour Relations Act (66 of 1995) and the Mine Health and Safety Act (29 of 1996). Some important features of these plain language statutes include the following:

- Important information is placed at the start, definitions at the end.
- "Must" replaces "shall".
- Defined words and phrases are written in italics.
- There is a clear table of contents.
- Less important matters are dealt with in schedules.

In exceptional cases South African judges have realised the need for plain language. In *SA Defence Union v Minister of Defence and Another* 1999 (3) BCLR 321 (T) Hartzenberg J had this to say about the definition of an "act of public protest" (in Section 126B of the Defence Act (44 of 1957)):

> The 255-word definition, in one sentence, of "act of public protest" is not easy to understand. By omitting words, which denote similar conduct or actions, I have reduced the definition to something a little more workable ...
>
> It is significant that the definition is not exhaustive. In my view the definition is wide enough to render a complaint by a member to his wife about for instance the insufficiency of a salary increase as a contravention of the section. In my view by doing so the member indicates private opposition in respect of the government policy of remuneration of members. That, in my view, can never be an act of public protest. Acts, which do not fall within the concept of public protest, have in the definition been classified as such. It follows then that the definition is too wide and therefore "overbroad". It is unconstitutional.

In another example, Wunsh J (in *Stassen v Stassen* 1997 2 SA 105 (W)) criticised aspects of the language in an action for divorce. See also *Southern Cape Car Rentals CC t/a Budget Rent A Car v Braun* 1998 4 SA 1192 (SCA).

## 1.3 Plain language and business

The business world has taken interesting and important initiatives. In this regard one may mention the work and publications of *Plain Business Writing*.

Another indication of the increased awareness of plain language is a recent application for direct access to the Constitutional Court on the basis that the language used in the civil procedure amounts to a violation of the right to free and equal access to courts.[1]

## 2 Conference and workshop

On 2 July 1999 the Faculty of Law, University of Pretoria, hosted the first academic conference and workshop on plain legal language in South Africa. The conference was attended by interested delegates from private and public spheres including government and business. The keynote address was given by Mark Adler, President of Clarity (UK). The South African branch of Clarity was launched at this conference.

Several speakers presented papers giving a perspective on the progress that had been made thus far in developing a plain language approach for South Africa. Workshops discussed strategies for developing plain language policies.

The conference focussed attention on the need for plain language in a country such as South Africa.

## 3 Overview of this book

This book is the first of its kind in South Africa. It brings together most of the papers delivered at the 1999 conference. In some respects it goes beyond the conference proceedings (as in the contributions by the editors, and the paper by Minister Dullah Omar). In some instances the oral presentations were transcribed and edited. This working method accounts for the "conversational" style of some contributions.

In **Part A**, a general introduction to the book, we highlight the fact that the plain language approach is taking root in South Africa.

---

1   See "Moeilike regstaal die beskuldigde in konstitusionele hof" 8 February 2000, *Beeld* 5.

**Plain Legal Language Conference & Workshop**
*Making South African law more accessible and understandable*
2 July 1999

08:30 Welcoming
Prof Duard Kleyn (Dean, Faculty of Law, University of Pretoria)

08:40 **Theme 1: Simplifying legal language:
Introduction and international context**
Chair: Christa van der Walt (Department of English,
Vista University)

08:40 "Current developments in the UK"
(Mark Adler, Chairperson: Clarity, UK)

09:10 "Plain language communication – approaches and challenges"
(Derrick Fine, Plain Language Consultant, Cape Town)

09:40 "Plain language in a multilingual society"
(Mariëtta Alberts, Secretary, Centre for Legal Terminology
in African Languages)

10:00 Questions and discussions

10:30 **Theme 2: Progress towards plain legal language in
South Africa**
Chair: Ellison Kahn (Professor of Law, University of
the Witwatersrand)

10:30 "The 1996 Constitution and other innovative drafting"
(Justice Johann van der Westhuizen, High Court, Pretoria)

11:00 "Plain language in the current practice of drafting"
(Enver Daniels, Chief State Law Adviser)

11:30 "The drafting of the new Labour Relations Act"
(Amanda Armstrong, Cheadle & Thompson, Johannesburg)

12:00 "Report on recent empirical research project"
(Frans Viljoen and Annelize Nienaber, University of Pretoria)

12:20 Questions and discussions

12:50 (Re) Launch of *Clarity SA*
Mark Adler

| | |
|---|---|
| 13:45 | **Theme 3: Plain legal language in business**<br>Chair: Shadrack Gutto (CALS, University of the Witwatersrand) |
| 13:45 | "The growing use of plain legal language in the SA business sector"<br>(Robert Gentle, Managing Director, Plain Business Writing) |
| 14:05 | "A practitioner's perspective: Leases in plain legal language"<br>(Chris Leppan, Legal Advisor, WesBank) |
| 14:25 | Questions and discussions |
| 14:40 | **Theme 4: Workshop – division into small groups**<br>A  Legislative drafting – Enver Daniels (facilitator)<br>(State law advisers, linguists, drafters)<br><br>B  Language used by lawyers – Amanda Armstrong (facilitator)<br>(Practitioners, students)<br><br>C  Language in business transactions – Robert Gentle (facilitator)<br>(Business lawyers, consumers)<br><br>D  The use of plain language in courts – Mark Adler (facilitator)<br>(Judges, magistrates, translators)<br><br>E  Multilingualism and plain legal language – Ria Mabule<br>(Department of African Languages, Vista University, facilitator)<br>(Non-English mother tongue speakers, linguists, translators)<br><br>F  Plain language and public legal education – Derrick Fine<br>(Plain Language Consultant, Cape Town, facilitator)<br>(NGOs, academics, students)<br><br>G  Plain language in the study of law – Shadrack Gutto (facilitator)<br>(Academics, students) |
| 15:30 | Workshop Plenary: What next?<br>Chair: Frans Viljoen<br><br>Report back from small groups<br><br>Questions and discussions<br><br>Recommendations / Plan of Action |
| 16:25 | Thanks, conclusion<br>Annelize Nienaber |

**Part B** is an introduction to the main features of plain language communication.

**Part C** sketches the advances of plain language internationally. After a brief introduction, the focus falls on Australia, the UK and the USA.

**Part D** charts some of the progress already made in South Africa. The first contribution (D.1), a speech which Minister Dullah Omar presented in 1995, was not part of the conference. As this speech is the clearest and most committed statement supporting plain language any South African politician has made, it has been included. Other contributions show how the plain language approach was used in drafting the 1996 Constitution (D.2), the Labour Relations Act (D.3) and how it has been used in the business sector (D.5). D.4 is an important contribution, as it gives previously undisclosed insights into the work of the state law advisers. D.6 is a comprehensive investigation into the co-existence of plain language and a multiplicity of languages.

In **Part E** we present the research results of a project entitled "Plain language for a multilingual South Africa". The National Research Foundation (NRF) sponsored this research.

**Part F**, the conclusion, speculates on future possibilities and catalogues the launching of Clarity's South African branch.

We hope that **Part G**, a list of some plain language sources, will be a helpful resource for those interested in reading or knowing more.

**Part H** offers a brief biographical background of the contributors.

## 4 Acknowledgement of financial support

The following institutions provided financial support:
- The National Research Foundation: Social Sciences and Humanities.
- The Faculty of Law, University of Pretoria.

> The financial assistance of the National Research Foundation: Social Sciences and Humanities towards this research is hereby acknowledged. Opinions expressed and conclusions arrived at are those of the authors and are not necessarily attributable to the National Research Foundation.

# B
# What is plain language?

B.1 Plain language communication: Approaches and challenges — page 19

## B.1
# Plain language communication: Approaches and challenges

**Derrick Fine**
*Training, Plain Language and Research Consultant*

> 1 Sharing a vision ... *page 19*
> 2 Context and barriers ... *page 20*
> 3 Defining plain language communication ... *page 20*
> 4 Summarising the benefits of plain language ... *page 22*
> 5 Plain language guidelines ... *page 23*
> 6 Examples of using a plain language approach ... *page 25*
> 7 Reaching our vision: key challenges ... *page 25*

In starting ...

Thanks to the University of Pretoria's Law Faculty and Centre for Human Rights for giving us this opportunity of sharing ideas and learnings from our experience of plain legal language work. I've been asked to give a background to plain language work, and then to suggest a few pointers for the future.

## 1 Sharing a vision

A proposed vision for plain language work:
> To develop the capacity of the community, NGO, government, legal and other professional sectors to communicate plainly and effectively.

## 2     Context and barriers

Context for making SA law more accessible and understandable:
- Making new language policy and multilingualism part of our everyday lives
- Improving communication and understanding – interpersonal, community and workplace
- Improving literacy and adult education
- Improving public education and human rights awareness

Barriers to more accessible / understandable law and legal services:
- Difficult legal language and procedures
- Educational levels and literacy
- Legal costs and delays
- Personal attitudes, for example intolerance, impatience, arrogance
- Environmental factors, for example offices, staff, dress, formality
- Language diversity and need for translation / interpretation
- Shortage of multilingual practitioners
- Need for appropriate equivalent terms in all languages

## 3     Defining plain language communication

### 3.1   "Plain language"

- Clear
- Understandable
- Accessible
- User-friendly

### 3.2   "Using plain language"

For readers and listeners at different levels:
> In all languages, writing and speaking at a level that most people can understand.

For specific readers and listeners:
> In all languages, writing or speaking at their level of understanding.

## 3.3 "A plain language approach to communication"

- Try to think of plain language as part of effective communication.
- Our challenge: to develop an effective plain language approach to communication.

> A PLAIN LANGUAGE APPROACH TO COMMUNICATION:
> 1. Understandable and informative *language*
>    AND
> 2. Clear and well-organised *structure*
> 3. Clear and user-friendly *layout* and *design* for written materials and visual backups when speaking
> 4. Appropriate and user-friendly *tone* in writing and *body language* when speaking

## 3.4 Plain language in all South African languages

- Plain language = *level* of language
- Translating/interpreting = *choice* of language
- Our challenge: to move away from the main focus on plain English to develop plain language guidelines and materials in all SA languages

*Step 1* Best approach: put into plain language *before* interpreting or translating
   Alternative approach: put into plain language *during* interpreting or translating

*Step 2* Keep in plain language in interpreted / translated language

> EXAMPLE WITH SPOKEN LANGUAGE:
> 1. Lawyer speaks in difficult legal language
> 2. Interpreter puts into plain language (in his/her head)
> 3. Interpreter interprets in plain language
> 4. Client listens and speaks
> 5. Interpreter conveys to lawyer in plain language

EXAMPLE WITH WRITTEN LANGUAGE:
1   Lawyer writes in difficult legal language
2   Plain language editor revises into plain language
3   Translator translates in plain language
4   Translation checked for consistency between languages

- Challenging the assumption: always writing in English as a *source* language and then translating from the English version.
- Key lessons:
  - Whenever possible, involve translators and interpreters early in the process.
  - At least, always fully brief translators and interpreters.

### 3.5 Plain language in all professions

- Need to apply plain language approach and principles to written and oral communication in all professional / paraprofessional disciplines and sectors.
- Examples: legal / paralegal, medical / paramedical, environmental, educational, business.

## 4 Summarising the benefits of plain language

- Better communication of information to all your readers and listeners.
- More involvement and participation from the people you want to reach.
- More understanding of your message, which makes it easier for people to pass on to others.
- Saving time and money because more people will need less help in knowing what they must do.

## 5 Plain language guidelines

### 5.1 Writing and speaking planning questions

WHY? – Purpose or aim
WHO? – Knowing my readers/listeners: level + choice of language
WHAT? – Information, amount of detail, structure + emphasis
HOW? – Methods, layout and design, tone + body language

### 5.2 Plain language speaking exercise

- Speaker: practise explaining a difficult legal concept, structure or procedure to a partner (= a non-legal member of the public).
- Listener: stop the speaker ("beep") each time he/she uses words or expressions you do not understand.
- Speaker: put the "beeped" words into plain language, using easier words or a practical example.

Use this exercise or roleplay your full input to get feedback from colleagues before you speak on new or difficult topics.

### 5.3 Degrees or levels of plainness

- Our aim: to draft documents and to speak in "plain" language.
- What we usually achieve: relative plainness or degrees of plainness, ie "plainer" language, an improvement on previous attempts – rather than perfect "plain" language.

THE PLAIN LANGUAGE CONTINUUM OR SCALE:

Difficult ●·······❯·······● Plainer ·······❯·······● Plain

- Key factors determining degree of plainness:
  - The answer to the "who" question: your readership / audience.
  - The complexity of the material.
  - Our plain language skill and experience.

### 5.4 Different plain language versions

Use your "who" and "what" planning questions to decide on detail and thus if you need to write a *full*, *summary* or *popular* plain language version:

FULL PLAIN LANGUAGE VERSION:
- Writing the whole original document in plain language.
- Communicating the full meaning of the original in a more readable way.

SUMMARY PLAIN LANGUAGE VERSION:
- Writing a summary of the original document in plain language.
- Communicating all the key ideas and points of the original in a shorter, more readable way.

POPULAR PLAIN LANGUAGE VERSION:
- Writing a short illustrated version of the original document in plain language.
- Communicating some of the key ideas of the original using a mixture of text, slogans, graphics and other accessible methods.

### 5.5 Some practical plain language tips

Develop and use helpful plain language writing and speaking guidelines wherever possible and appropriate, for example:
- Decide which difficult or technical words are necessary.
- Explain difficult/technical words and abbreviations, for example easier words, examples, personal experiences, a definition box or glossary.
- Avoid unnecessary difficult, technical, foreign or outdated words.
- Cut all extra words which add nothing to your meaning.
- Use the active voice, not the passive voice.
- Use the first and second person, not the third person.
- Break up into digestible pieces, for example "one idea, one sentence", "one theme, one paragraph".

- Order and structure logically, for example numbering, headings.
- Show or explain your structure, for example contents, outline.
- Design creatively and appropriately, eg:
  - Illustrations and less text for people with low literacy.
  - Larger font and open spaces for people with impaired sight.

## 6 Examples of using a plain language approach

- Drafting White Papers and other policy documents.
- Drafting Bills and Acts.
- Writing summaries of policy documents and legislation.
- Writing public and adult education materials, for example pamphlets, booklets, information-sheets, manuals, course-books.
- Drafting a variety of other documents, for example letters, contracts, constitutions, reports, conditions of service, application forms.
- Training lawyers, para-legals, government officials and NGOs in plain language and effective communication skills for:
  - Writing legal and official documents.
  - Advising and reporting to clients and the public.
  - Telephone speaking.
  - Public speaking.
  - Running workshops and seminars.
  - Developing community education materials.

## 7 Reaching our vision: key challenges

Personal challenges:
- Help develop an awareness of the need for plain language communication.
- Develop and apply our own plain language skills.
- Advise and encourage lawyers, para-legals, other professionals and colleagues to write and talk in plain language.

- Help to change attitudes and "mindsets" that resist plain language (especially plain language writing).
- Develop our ability to communicate in more South African languages.

Collective challenges:
- Share and further develop plain language writing and speaking guidelines, and training materials.
- Share and develop "before and after" successful plain language examples as models for training and lobbying.
- Network and run joint training of lawyers, para-legals, law students, interpreters, court officials and other role players.
- Co-operate on targeted pilot programmes, for example legislative drafting, plain language capacity-building in specific sectors.
- Lobby to integrate plain language and effective communication skills training into existing curricula, for example in schools, university law schools, practical legal training, paralegal training, continuing legal education.
- Build human rights awareness and gender sensitivity into plain language and effective communication skills training.
- Network and co-operate to specially focus on plain language public education materials and interactive methods (like drama and community radio) as the most direct way of reaching people.
- Co-operate on applying plain language guidelines to all South African languages and developing specific further guidelines needed for particular languages.
- Co-operate with initiatives to develop equivalent legal terminology in all South African languages – for both technical and plain language use.
- Network with initiatives to apply a plain language approach in other disciplines and professions, for example business sector.

In closing …

- Let's continue to raise the plain language flag!
- Let's use today's space to develop effective joint initiatives!

# C
# What's happening? Plain language in the international context

C.1 Introduction — page 29
C.2 Plain language in Australia: An overview — page 31
C.3 Current developments in the UK — page 36
C.4 The plain language experience in the USA — page 45

## C.1
# Introduction

**Frans Viljoen**
*Faculty of Law, University of Pretoria*

**Annelize Nienaber**
*Faculty of Law, University of Pretoria*

Contributions to this book focus on developments in plain language. The modern plain language movement started in the United States of America (USA). Other countries soon followed suit, sometimes with greater vigour and success than the United States. Plain legal language is used today most frequently in Australia, Canada, New Zealand and the United Kingdom.

The three contributions that follow on Australia, the UK and the USA do not aim to give a systematic or comprehensive overview of developments in these countries. Rather, the contributions indicate trends and illustrate what has been achieved by means of examples.

Although we do not include a discussion of developments in Canada, we must emphasise that the plain language movement has been very active in Canada. The work of the Plain Language Institute of British Columbia (replaced in 1993 by a plain language programme in the Ministry of Government Services) should be mentioned. Other examples are the Plain English Local Government Bill for Alberta and the plain language programme in Saskatchewan.

In other countries where English is the (or **a** major) language of the law, plain language approaches have also gained ground. There are references to seminars or workshops on topics relating to plain language in India, Ireland, Japan, Papua New Guinea, Singapore, Spain and Sweden in previous issues of *Clarity*.

Significant advances in plain language have been made in Sweden. Initiatives date back to 1965. The Prime Minister's Office initiated projects to vet legislation and later appointed a linguist to the Office. Since 1980 a team of language experts has been revising drafts before their presentation to the Swedish parliament. The Ordinance for the Ministries 1982 prescribes that departments must ensure that "all statutes and decisions are written in a clear and simple language". In the mid-990s, the Swedish government appointed a Plain Language Committee to encourage state agencies to start plain language projects. This Committee remains active.

Greater economic, political and legal unity in Europe increasingly necessitates a common language. English is the first language of only two of the European Union member states (UK and Ireland), but is fast becoming the major shared means of communication. The bureaucratic tendencies of the European institutions require plain language. The plain language movement may have much to contribute in this regard.

## C.2
# Plain language in Australia: An overview

**Annelize Nienaber**
*Faculty of Law, University of Pretoria*

---

1   Introduction ... *page 31*
2   The role of the Law Reform Commission ... *page 32*
3   The Centre for Plain Legal Language ... *page 32*
4   Plain Language Committees and Plain Language Units ... *page 33*
5   Legislative incentives ... *page 33*
6   Current developments ... *page 34*

---

## 1   Introduction

In an address to a conference of New South Wales Supreme Court judges on 30 April 1993, the Chief Justice of Australia, Sir Anthony Mason, stressed the importance of using a clear and easily comprehensible style of writing:

> Unfortunately, judgements do not speak in a language or style that people readily understand. [...] The lesson to be learnt is that, if we want people to understand what we are doing, we should write in a way that makes it possible for them to do so.

The realisation that judges need to write in an easily comprehensible style in order to be accessible, voiced by Australia's chief justice, shows the progress that has been made in Australia in raising awareness of plain language issues. Some of the most significant developments in plain language have taken place in Australia. In Australia the debate around the need for plain language began in the seventies.

## 2   The role of the Law Reform Commission

The Law Reform Commission of Victoria has been pivotal in the plain English movement in Australia and has contributed significantly to introducing plain English into the drafting of legislation and other legal documents. The Law Reform Commission was created by an act of the Victoria Parliament in 1984. It is estimated that about 20 per cent of its law reform work has been devoted to work on plain language and the greater accessibility of the law.

## 3   The Centre for Plain Legal Language

In 1990, the Centre for Plain Legal Language was established as a joint project of the Law Foundation of New South Wales and the Faculty of Law, University of Sydney. The Centre was established with the exclusive aim of researching the use of plain language. In one of its first projects, the Centre was involved in investigating the costs and benefits of introducing plain language documents. It has made a substantial contribution to research into different aspects of legal English, and also provided aid in the drafting of documents and legislation in plain English.

The Centre for Plain Legal Language also produced a report on the design of legislation. This report recommended substantial changes to the design and layout of legislation, in an effort to improve readability. These recommendations have subsequently been adopted by drafters in New South Wales and other jurisdictions.

One of the Centre's best-known activities was the monthly "words and phrases" column that it published in the *New South Wales Law Society Journal*. Each month, the Centre would take a well-known legal term, research its meaning as it developed through caselaw, and suggest a plain language alternative that could serve as an adequate replacement for the original term. This column not only showed which plain language terms were "safe" to use in legal documents, but also succeeded in bringing plain language to the attention of the legal profession in Australia.

Although no longer in existence, the Centre played an invaluable role in increasing awareness in the legal profession, government and private industry of the benefits of using plain language.

The work of the Centre for Plain Legal Language is being continued by institutions such as the Communication Research Institute of Australia. This Institute is a non-profit organisation that specialises in information design. It not only undertakes independent research, but also translates documents such as Australia's Tax Form S into plain English.

## 4 Plain Language Committees and Plain Language Units

Another important development had been the establishment of Plain Language Committees in the Law Societies of several states in Australia. These societies have managed to bring about change from within the legal profession.

A number of leading Australian law firms have set up "plain language units" to produce plain language precedents. These law firms invest large amounts of money in plain language and readily promote themselves as plain language firms. Smaller firms have to follow suit in order to be competitive.

## 5 Legislative incentives

Recent legislative changes have given further momentum to the plain language movement in Australia. A number of states – notably New South Wales, Victoria and Queensland – produce plain language legislation. The New South Wales Local Government Act uses not only plain language, but also boxes and charts to help get its message across to its readers.

In 1994, the Industrial Relations Reform Act came into force. This Act compels the Industrial Relations Commission to write its awards in plain language. The Consumer Credit Code, which came into effect in 1996, prescribes a plain language content and design for documents relating to the granting of consumer credit.

Currently, Australia's federal government is involved in drafting Australia's tax and corporate law in plain language. Many sections of the Corporations' Law redraft have already been passed into law. In one instance the Corporations' Law task force has managed to reduce the number of words in a part of the Corporations Law by 13 000 words.

In his article, "Rewriting Australia's Income Tax Law", K E Jones mentions a number of examples where the Income Tax Law Improvement Project task force was able to make significant plain language changes to the previously very cumbersome Australian

tax law. The main aim of the task force was to reduce the cost of complying with the income tax law by simplifying the law. The task force decided to rewrite the law completely, incorporating a new structure, numbering system and mode of expression. Use was made of summaries, signposts and "mind-mapping" to orientate the reader towards the material. The numbering system was greatly simplified. In terms of the presentation of concepts, care was taken to present information clearly:
- Provisions are structured so that they do not exceed the limits of the readers short-term memory capacity.
- Emphasis is placed on underlying principles which are separated from qualifications and exceptions.
- Prominence is given in a sentence to the verb, which contains the central idea.

Unlike practices in the past where original "legal English" documents were re-drafted or translated into plain language only after the original had been drafted in "legal language", drafters are now able to draft tax and corporate legislation directly in plain language. In such cases, the plain language document is the original document used by the public, the courts and the legal profession, and not a mere secondary translation.

## 6  Current developments

Today, most major banks, insurance companies, law firms and local government departments in Australia employ plain language specialists who draft all consumer documents in plain language. In many instances, advertising campaigns boast the use of plain language documents to attract members of the public.

Significant examples of Australia's implementation of plain language tenets are the following:
- Several Australian banks have drawn up plain language mortgages, leases and guarantees.
- The family court of Australia is reviewing all its forms in an attempt to make these more user-friendly to both clients of the court and its staff.
- To help registrars of the Supreme Court produce more comprehensible decisions, the Judicial Commission of New South Wales has offered a workshop on Decision Writing for Registrars of the Supreme Court;

- In a discussion paper by the Trade Practices Commission, the Commission recommended that contracts in the building industry be in plain English.
- In *Clear Legislative Drafting: New Approaches in Australia*, Ian Turnbull QC, illustrates how the style of drafting in Australia's parliament has changed:
  > In a section with several subsections, the traditional practice is to bind the later ones to the earlier ones by expressions like "an application made by a corporation under subsection (1) …" In such a case we should simply say "an application …"

Recently, attention has also been given to the initiation of law students to plain language drafting. At some law faculties in Australia, programmes are being introduced to teach students plain language drafting at undergraduate level. It is intended that future generations of Australian lawyers will consider plain language drafting as the only useful way of communicating.

## C.3
# Current developments in the UK

**Mark Adler**
*Chairman, Clarity*

---

1   History ... *page 36*
2   Commerce ... *page 38*
3   Statutes ... *page 38*
4   Courts ... *page 41*
5   Practising lawyers in general ... *page 42*
6   Local government ... *page 44*
7   What do the clients think? ... *page 44*

---

## 1    History

A thousand years ago wills were written in plain Anglo-Saxon. From then until recently legal language deteriorated steadily. One contributing factor was the importation of languages and the custom of using a synonym from each (for example, *give* (English), *devise* (French), and *bequeath* (Latin)). For a detailed, scholarly and very readable history of legal English from Roman to modern times, I strongly recommend Professor David Mellinkoff's *The Language of the Law* 1963 (Aspen Publishers Inc, 7201 McKinney Circle, Frederick, Maryland 21704 ($36.10)).

Over the centuries there were occasional rebellions, but none was of much consequence. Some of you will know the story of the 16th century Lord Chancellor who had a verbose lawyer's client paraded around Westminster Hall with his head through a hole in his 120-page pleadings. It should of course have been the lawyer's head, but even in those days the bar looked after its own.

We might trace the modern English beginning of plain legal language back to Parker's *Conveyancing* and *Wills Precedents* in the late 1960s. Parker acknowledges the influence of Reed Dickerson, who had been teaching plain legal drafting at Indiana University in the States since the 2$^{nd}$ World War. Parker is still in print, but his work did not really take hold.

Sir Ernest Gowers had been promoting plain English in the civil service, but regrettably expressed the view in his *Complete Plain Words* that his strictures did not apply to legal language. He did not justify that remark, which is, of course, untenable.

It was the Plain English Campaign which started the revolution as opposed to a rebellion; and it came not from lawyers but from the public. The Campaign was a partnership between Martin Cutts, a journalist, and Chrissie Maher, a woman who had been illiterate until the age of 18 and has since campaigned vigorously for ordinary people to be allowed – even expected – to understand the documents that affect them. Neither had any legal training but Cutts has become a skilled drafter and they were, and still are, exceptionally effective publicists and lobbyists. The Plain English Campaign is still much better known in England than Clarity, although in my view it has not been the same organisation since Cutts's acrimonious departure in the 1980s. Cutts has set up the rival *Plain Language Commission,* and both organisations train professionals, government employees and businesspeople to write plainly; they both provide drafting services, and give their seal of approval to well-written documents. Clarity offers the same services but is restricted to legal drafting; virtually all our members are connected with the law, though we do have a sprinkling of interested outsiders.

The Plain English Campaign must take the credit for Margaret Thatcher's initiative in redrafting many government forms and booklets through the 1980s. Sadly, this project was quietly buried when John Major succeeded her in 1990.

When Clarity started in England in 1983 we were looked on as eccentrics by other lawyers. I was going to say that there was strong resistance to our views from the legal profession, but that would imply that our views were taken seriously. At about that time I sent out a draft lease to the solicitor for a prospective tenant and received it back with every punctuation mark neatly deleted in red. That would not happen now. Plain English drafts are generally welcomed by professional colleagues, even by those who do not write them themselves, as they know that they reduce the amount of work – much of it tedious – involved in transactions.

Now the principle that legal documents should be plain has become accepted by the establishment. The Law Society's 1990 book on legal drafting – *Clarity for Lawyers* – is devoted to plain language, and the Society has tried, though with only mixed success, to establish plain language precedents; it has accredited Clarity's seminars for its continuing education programme, and sometimes it seeks our help in drafting its own documents and training its own drafters. We have to a lesser extent had support from the Bar Council.

## 2    Commerce

Big business has been some way ahead of the legal profession. As in Australia, insurance companies took an early lead in using plain language as a selling point. Now one of our largest mortgage lenders has followed with an extensive TV advertising campaign promoting themselves on the basis that they use plain language "because life is complicated enough".

All businesses were given a push towards plain language by the Unfair Terms in Consumer Contract Regulations 1994. This is one of the few good things imposed on us by the European Community. The main purpose of the regulations, as their name suggests, is to outlaw unfair terms, paragraph 6 states:

> A seller or supplier shall ensure that any written term of a contract is expressed in plain, intelligible language, and if there is doubt about the meaning of a written term, the interpretation most favourable to the consumer shall prevail.

Happily, the regulations are now being rapidly enforced by the Office of Fair Trading, which publishes bulletins with before-and-after versions of the clauses it has persuaded businesses to rewrite. It has the power to extract undertakings, and to go to court for an injunction in default.

## 3    Statutes

Over the decades the style of British legislation has been slowly improving. The drafting has always – at least in my lifetime – been clearer than the documents typically produced by lawyers in private practice.

There too the revolution is taking hold. First parliamentary counsel, Christopher Jenkins QC, is a member of Clarity and there is widespread support for plain language principles among his staff. Our journal is passed around the office. However, his staff are constrained by the formal requirements of parliament and by the enormous pressure under which they work.

One exceptional piece of drafting is the Arbitration Act 1996. This has an interesting history. Although it was written by second parliamentary counsel, the first draft was prepared by an unusual team: a young junior barrister and Lord Justice Saville (who has since been promoted to the House of Lords). All used remarkably – though not perfect – plain English.

The Act begins with a statement of "general principles" – a purpose clause:

1. The provisions of this Part are founded on the following principles, and shall be construed accordingly –
   (a) the object of arbitration is to obtain the fair resolution of disputes by an impartial tribunal without unnecessary delay or expense;
   (b) the parties should be free to agree how their disputes are resolved, subject only to such safeguards as are necessary in the public interest;
   (c) in matters governed by this Part the court should not intervene except as provided by this Part.

An old-fashioned "shall" has crept into the first line (and into other parts of the Act), but in other places it has been replaced by a simple present tense. Compare the style of the 1996 Act with the Arbitration Act 1950:

**1950**
10. In any of the following cases –
    (a) where an arbitration agreement provides that the reference shall be to a single arbitrator, and all the parties do not, after differences have arisen, concur in the appointment of an arbitrator;
    (b) if an appointed arbitrator refuses to act, or is incapable of acting, or dies, and the arbitration agreement does not show that it was intended that the vacancy should not be supplied and the parties do not supply the vacancy;
    (c) where the parties or two arbitrators are required or are at liberty to appoint an umpire or third arbitrator and do not appoint him;
    (d) where an appointed umpire or third arbitrator refuses to act, or is incapable of acting, or dies, and the arbitration agreement does not show that it was intended that the

vacancy should not be supplied and the parties do not supply the vacancy;

any party may serve the other parties or the arbitrators, as the case may be, with a written notice to appoint or, as the case may be, concur in appointing, an arbitrator, umpire or third arbitrator, and if the appointment is not made within seven clear days after the service of the notice, the High Court or a Judge thereof may, on application by the party who gave the notice, appoint an arbitrator, umpire or third arbitrator who shall have the like powers to act in the reference, and make an award as if he had been appointed by consent of all parties.

**1996**

21 (1) Where the parties have agreed there is to be an umpire, they are free to agree what the functions of the umpire are to be, and in particular–
 (a) whether he is to attend the proceedings, and
 (b) whether he is to replace the other arbitrators as the tribunal with power to make decisions, orders and awards.

(2) If or to the extent that there is no such agreement, the following provisions apply.

(3) ...

But the greatest single current development is the Inland Revenue's project to rewrite all our tax legislation "in clearer, simpler language". The initiative was announced in 1996 by the then (Conservative) Chancellor of the Exchequer and it is continuing, with all-party support, under the Labour administration. It was to take five years with an annual budget of five million pounds. There has been extensive consultation on issues of style and policy, with before-and-after drafts offered for comment. Predictably, it is taking much longer than expected, and we are still awaiting the first legislation, the Capital Allowances Bill, but the Inland Revenue and parliamentary counsel's offices are dedicated to the project and have the support of the tax community (including tax lawyers). Consultation documents are posted on the government's website at www.Inlandrevenue.gov.uk.

Here is a flavour from an early draft Bill:

*Introduction*

### 3.1.1 Income taxed as trading income

(1) Tax is charged under this Part on the profits of a trade, profession or vocation.

(2) Chapter 3.2 contains rules about how to calculate profits for this purpose.

(3) This Part is drafted in terms of trades and trading but unless otherwise indicated the provisions of this Part apply equally to professions and vocations.

### 3.1.2 Trading income of UK residents

(1) If a UK resident carries on a trade wholly or partly in the United Kingdom, tax is charged under this Part on profits arising to that person from that trade, wherever it is carried on.

(2) Profits arising to a UK resident from a trade carried on wholly outside the United Kingdom are taxed under Part 9 (foreign income).

### 3.1.3 Trading income of non-UK residents

(1) Tax is charged under this Part on profits arising to a non-UK resident from a trade carried on in the United Kingdom as follows.

(2) If the trade is carried on wholly in the United Kingdom, tax is charged on all the profits arising from the trade.

(3) If the trade is carried on partly in the United Kingdom and partly elsewhere, tax is charged on the profits arising from the trade to the extent that they arise from the part of the trade carried on in the United Kingdom.

*Meaning of "trade"*

### 3.1.4 Meaning of "trade"

(1) In this Act trade includes every venture in the nature of trade.

(2) An activity may amount to a trade although the profits are earned wholly or partly from the occupation of land or the exploitation of land or its natural resources. Such activities are not taxed under this Part if, or to the extent that, they are taxed under Part 5 (income from land).

(3) This section does not apply to professions and vocations.

# 4 Courts

Before considering plain language in the courts we should be aware of the distinction between documents giving rise to litigation and documents created for litigation. Should we take it for granted that the same attitudes will apply to both?

Judges have long criticised the drafting of documents which have provoked litigation. For example:
- 19th century criticism of "and/or".
- L J Saville's conclusion to his 1994 Court of Appeal judgment in *Trafalgar House Construction v. General Surety & Guarantee Co* (66 Building Law Reports 47):

  I would only add a suggestion both to those who seek and to those who provide securities for the performance of commercial obligations. They would save much time and money if in future they heeded what Lord Atkin had said so many years ago and set out their bargain in plain modern English without resorting to ancient forms which were doubtless designed for legal reasons which no longer exist.

As far as I know, no judge has ever penalised a document because it was written in plain language (though of course badly written plain-type English will be open to criticism). On the contrary, I have found plain language pleadings and witness statements a considerable help in achieving good results. And of course a clearly written document will not provoke litigation over its meaning.

Sadly, most judges write the same legalese as they did when they were in practice and see no need to discourage lawyers from following their bad example. But a few (mostly in the senior ranks) actively encourage plain language.

The Civil Procedure Rules, which came into force on 26 April, are the first substantial stage in bringing the plain language revolution into the courts. The rules for most civil actions have been dramatically rationalised, and are plainly written. We wait to see whether it has much effect on litigation lawyers' drafting; I suspect that will take some time and further reform.

## 5    Practising lawyers in general

In 1992 I sent a questionnaire to 150 solicitors, 66 junior barristers, and 19 silks: 56 replied, spread over the three groups. As they were lawyers, I am afraid it was rather difficult to make sense of their replies, but it seemed that the blame for legalese could be apportioned between fear and ignorance. We have moved on a bit since 1992, but not so much that the results are no longer interesting.

Only one respondent said that he did not support the use of plain English by lawyers.

When asked if they used plain English themselves, only four said "no". Ninety-three per cent answered "yes" or "maybe". But when we tested their understanding of the basic principles of plain English, we found that 47 of the 56 had no idea what was involved. There was no objection to sentences of 100 words or more, or to the use of passive verbs when an active one would do. On the other hand, there was virtual unanimity in their adherence to cosmetic rules (barring split infinitives, and not ending a sentence with a preposition). Surprisingly, eighty-nine per cent favoured punctuation in all documents.

## 5.1    Large solicitors' firms

I've been told – but do not know the details – that all the big city firms are now making an effort to switch to plain language. This is a very recent development. I know of a couple of firms who are taking the initiative seriously and there are probably others, but they all have to struggle against the resistance and habits of traditionally trained partners and staff. There is a general tendency to shorter sentences, but I rarely see anything that could seriously be mistaken for plain language. The last Clarity awards, a couple of years ago, produced as entries a lot of "notes for clients", but when I asked if they could not submit a formal document in plain language they merely looked embarrassed. (For this year's awards we have banned informal documents.) I think we will notice a significant improvement over the next few years but traditionally drafted documents are still the norm.

## 5.2    Small solicitors' firms

Change here is even slower. The large firms can set up redrafting teams and in-house training, but the smaller ones do not have the resources. However, they do tend to appreciate receiving plain documents, realising that it makes their work easier. This is a considerable change: they now almost universally accept that plain is good, so long as they do not have to write it.

## 5.3    The bar

Like the small solicitors' firms the generalisation – and I speak only from my own limited impressions – is that barristers have heard about plain English and understand it is the coming thing, but would rather not have to worry about it before they have to. Rather like tax.

## 6   Local government

Development in local government is patchy. Some years ago I put on a plain drafting workshop for a local authority's legal department whose head was a long-standing member of Clarity. It was enthusiastically received. Quite recently I discovered that they were still routinely sending out traditionally drafted documents.

I have had particular difficulty with inner city authorities, which tend to have severe funding problems. They cut corners by employing underqualified people, and sometimes not even the head of the legal department is a lawyer. Morale tends to be low. There is no initiative. They refuse to allow their standard, badly written, precedents to be amended even when it is pointed out that they do not make sense, or are inaccurate.

## 7   What do the clients think?

Clients love plain language, and it is an excellent selling point for your practice. A typical comment is: "How wonderful! I can understand it." And there are practical advantages for lawyers: clients can vet draft documents properly and pick up mistakes in time to correct them; and if they miss a mistake there is less chance of us, the lawyers, being held responsible.

An unexceptional letter from a solicitor to his client's estranged wife, circulated for comment to a group of lay people, stimulated a barrage of abuse and unanimous condemnation, including:
- Stuffy as well as unclear
- A general woolliness
- Sly
- Prolix
- I get a nasty feeling I might be missing out on something
- It is verbose without containing the necessary information
- The style is appalling ... arrogant
- Pompous, platitudinous, cliché-ridden.

## C.4
# The plain language experience in the USA[1]

**Frans Viljoen**
*Faculty of Law, University of Pretoria*

---

1 Document Design Center ... *page 45*
2 Plain language laws ... *page 46*
3 Veterans Benefits Administration ... *page 46*
4 Federal administrative regulations ... *page 47*
5 Security and Exchange Commission ... *page 47*
6 Supreme Court Rules ... *page 48*
7 Presidential memorandum: June 1998 ... *page 49*
8 Since the 1998 memorandum ... *page 50*
9 Conclusion ... *page 51*

---

The modern Plain Language Movement started in the 1970s in the United States of America (USA). Despite a period of inactivity in the 1980s, the Movement gained renewed momentum in the late 1990s. What follows is a discussion of some of the most significant gains of the Movement.

## 1 Document Design Center

In 1978, the government funded a Document Design Project to improve clear writing and design in public documents. A Document Design Center was set up. One of its publications is *Guidelines for Document Designers*. This guide influenced many drafters to improve documents. Unfortunately, the Center is now inactive.

---

1 This contribution relies heavily on articles in (1997) 38 *Clarity*, (1998) 42 *Clarity*, (1999) 44 *Clarity* and (1996) *Campaign International*, the magazine of the Plain English Campaign.

## 2 Plain language laws

A number of states have adopted laws requiring certain consumer documents to be written in plain English. New Jersey, for example, adopted a Plain Language Act in 1980. The law requires that consumer contracts have to be written in "a simple, clear, understandable and easily readable way". The law applies to all consumer contracts, defined as amongst others, "a written agreement in which an individual (a) leases or licences real or personal property; (b) obtains credit". A consumer is entitled to compensation for actual damage caused by non-compliance "if the violation caused the consumer to be substantially confused about the rights, obligations or remedies of the contract". By 1995, nine states (Connecticut, Hawaii, Maine, Minnesota, Montana, New Jersey, New York, West Virginia and Pennsylvania) had adopted legislation necessitating plain language in consumer contracts.

Other states require that insurance policies be written in plain language.

## 3 Veterans Benefits Administration

The Veterans Benefits Administration (VBA) was not known for its clear language. Rather, it had a reputation for processing benefits slowly. Many veterans also complained that they were unable to understand the VBA's letters.

In the 1990s, the VBA launched a Reader-Focused Writing (RFW) initiative. With this programme, the VBA set out to train many of its 8 000 staff members all over the USA to write clearly. Training was done by means of satellites as well as through other methods. Staff members started to apply the principles of plain English in all communications. An important feature of RFW is that users test letters and manuals before the VBA uses the letters and manuals more widely. The VBA built up material and other resources. A formal review showed that veterans reacted positively to RFW's plain language approach.

The following is an example of how the VBA has improved its communications. Here is the "before" example:

> We are providing the following information about an insurance payment you indicate you have not received or which is otherwise missing. We have given the Treasury Department the necessary information to trace the check in question.

The new version is:
> We received the missing-check form you sent us. We asked the Treasury Department to find out what happened to it.

The RFW initiative had an important ripple effect. It has improved the morale of staff members, leaving them feeling that they are doing their jobs well and meaningfully.

## 4   Federal administrative regulations

Under President Clinton the federal government embarked on an earnest campaign to start using plain English in its administration. The President's Executive Order 12866 (30 September 1993) was a seminal event. The Order included the following directive: "Each agency shall draft its regulations to be simple and easy to understand, with a goal of minimising the potential for uncertainty and litigation arising from such uncertainty." In a further memorandum (4 March 1995) President Clinton urged heads of departments to conduct a review of all regulations.

As a resulting example, the Occupational Safety and Health Administration changed its guidelines for leaving a building in a hurry. What before were called "Means of Egress" are now called "Exit Routes".

## 5   Security and Exchange Commission

In January 1998, the Security and Exchange Commission (SEC) announced new rules calling for plain English in prospectuses. The new rules apply only to prospectuses provided by public companies to prospective investors in the sale of securities. The SEC also released a *Plain English Handbook*. Here is an example from the SEC's handbook:

> **Use concrete rather than abstract words.**
> *Before:* The markets for certain of the Machine Tools Inc products historically have been highly cyclical, characterized by periods of supply and demand imbalance.
> *After:* The markets for some of our products vary dramatically. In the past, we have seen sharp increases and decreases in orders for our products.

## 6  Supreme Court Rules

On 24 April 1998, the US Supreme Court approved a new set of rules for federal appellate courts. However, these rules were changed to improve their **style** and not to affect **substantive** provisions. In the early 1990s, work started on the Civil Rules, but was stalled. The idea grew that the Appellate Rules, being less controversial than the Civil Rules, were a better starting point for a wholesale stylistic rewrite.

Here is an example of a "before" and "after" rule:

**Rule 18. Stay Pending Review**

Application for a stay of a decision or order of any agency pending direct review in the court of appeals shall ordinarily be made in the first instance to the agency. A motion for such relief may be made to the court of appeals or to a judge thereof, but the motion shall show that the application to the agency for the relief sought is not practicable, or that application has been made to the agency and denied, with the reasons given by it for denial, or that the action of the agency did not afford the relief which the application had requested. The motion shall also show the reasons for the relief requested and the facts relied upon and if the facts are subject to dispute the motion shall be supported by affidavits or other sworn statements or copies thereof. With the motion shall be filed such parts of the record as are relevant to the relief sought. Reasonable notice of the motion shall be given to all parties to the proceeding in the court of appeals. The court may condition relief under this rule upon the filing of a bond or other appropriate security. The motion shall be filed with the clerk and normally will be considered by a panel or division of the court, but in exceptional cases where such procedure would be impracticable due to the requirements of time, the application may be made to and considered by a single judge of the court.

**Rule 18. Stay Pending Review**
*(a) Motion for a Stay*
(1) **Initial Motion Before the Agency.** A petitioner must ordinarily move first before the agency for a stay pending review of its decision or order.
(2) **Motion in the Court of Appeals.** A motion for a stay may be made to the court of appeals or one of its judges.
  (A) The motion must:
     (i) show that moving first before the agency would be impracticable; or
     (ii) state that, a motion having been made, the agency denied the motion or failed to afford the relief requested and state any reasons given by the agency for its actions.

(B) The motion must also include:
  (i) the reasons for granting the relief requested and the facts relied on;
  (ii) originals or copies of affidavits or other sworn statements supporting facts subject to dispute; and
  (iii) relevant parts of the record.
(C) The moving party must give reasonable notice of the motion to all parties.
(D) The motion must be filed with the circuit clerk and normally will be considered by a panel of the court. But in an exceptional case in which time requirements make that procedure impracticable, the motion may be made to and considered by a single judge.
  *(b) Bond:* The court may condition relief on the filing of a bond or other appropriate security.

## 7   Presidential memorandum: June 1998

On 1 June 1998 President Clinton issued a memorandum on plain language. It formed part of the National Partnership for Reinventing Government. The memorandum has given new life to the plain language movement. The full text of the memorandum follows:

**MEMORANDUM FOR THE HEADS OF EXECUTIVE DEPARTMENTS AND AGENCIES**

SUBJECT: Plain Language in Government Writing

The Vice President and I have made reinventing the Federal Government a top priority of my Administration. We are determined to make the Government more responsive, accessible, and understandable in its communications with the public.

The Federal Government's writing must be in plain language. By using plain language, we send a clear message about what the Government is doing, what it requires, and what services it offers. Plain language saves the Government and the private sector time, effort, and money.

Plain language requirements vary from one document to another, depending on the intended audience. Plain language documents have a logical organisation, easy-to-read-design features, and use:
- Common, everyday words, except for necessary technical terms;
- "you" and other pronouns;
- the active voice; and
- short sentences.

To ensure the use of plain language, I direct you to the following:

- By October 1, 1998, use plain language in all new documents, other than regulations, that explain how to obtain a benefit or service or how to comply with a requirement you administer or enforce. For example, these documents may include letters, forms, notices, and instructions. By January 1, 2002, all such documents created prior to October 1, 1998, must also be in plain language.
- By January 1, 1999, use plain language in all proposed and final rulemaking documents published in the *Federal Register*, unless you proposed the rule before that date. You should consider rewriting existing regulations in plain language when you have the opportunity and resources to do so.

The National Partnership for Reinventing Government will issue guidance to help you comply with these directives and to explain more fully the elements of plain language. You should also use customer feedback and common sense to guide your plain language efforts.

I ask independent agencies to comply with these directives.

This memorandum does not confer any right or benefit enforceable by law against the United States or its representatives. The Director of the Office of Management and Budget will publish this memorandum in *Federal Register*.

## 8 Since the 1998 memorandum

Since June 1998, the federal government has made progress.[2] This includes the following:

- The VBA has continued its efforts. In June 1999, it trained 8 000 of its 13 000 employees to write for the reader.
- The Food and Drug Administration (FDA) now requires manufacturers of over-the-counter drugs to label these drugs in clear language.
- The Federal Aviation Authority (FAA) is now ensuring that regulations about aviation safety are in plain language.[3]
- Many other agencies (federal government departments) have introduced plain language training of staff members.

---

2 See <www.plainlanguage.gov>.
3 See <www.faa.gov/language>.

## 9  Conclusion

Academics and practitioners have encouraged and reinforced government initiatives. *The Scribes Journal of Legal Writing* fosters plain language in legal writing. Columns on plain writing appear in several state law journals (eg Michigan, Florida, Colorado). The Bar associations of three states (Michigan, Pennsylvania, Missouri) have established plain language committees. The Committee on Communication Skills sponsored a programme on plain language writing at the 1995 Annual Meeting of the American Bar Association. Two academics who have been very prominent are Professor Joe Kimble (Thomas Cooley Law School) and Bryan A Garner (Dallas, Texas, editor of *The Scribes Journal of Legal Writing*).

Plain language has made a significant contribution to the administration of law in the USA. Future challenges lie in extending plain language to legislative drafting.

# D
# Plain legal language in South Africa

D.1 Plain language, the law and the right to information — page 55
D.2 Plain language in the drafting of the
1996 Constitution — page 61
D.3 Some concise guidelines to the process of drafting the new
Labour Relations Act in plain language — page 71
D.4 Plain language in the current practice of drafting — page 78
D.5 A practitioner's perspective: Leases in plain language — page 86
D.6 Plain language in a multilingual society — page 89

## D.1
# Plain language, the law and the right to information

**Dullah Omar**
*Minister of Justice*[1]

> 1 Introduction ... *page 55*
> 2 Access to justice ... *page 56*
> 3 Participatory democracy ... *page 57*
> 4 Multilingual society ... *page 58*
> 5 Literacy ... *page 59*
> 6 Conclusion ... *page 60*

Opening address by the South African Minister of Justice, Mr Dullah Omar, at a seminar hosted by the Ministry of Justice and sponsored by the British High Commission and British Council, 10 March 1995[2]

## 1 Introduction

It is with great pleasure that I welcome you all to this seminar on *Plain language, the law and the right to information*. I believe this to be an important milestone in our vision for a transformed justice system. I hope, too, that the discussions we have here today will mark a beginning of many efforts in government to address, in a practical way, the right to information enshrined in our Constitution.

We are very grateful to the five plain language experts who have come from England, Australia, Canada and the United States to share their knowledge and their experiences with us. It has been deeply encouraging to learn that the campaign for plain language is one that has taken root in and brought so much benefit to their countries. It has given us faith that, here too, we may achieve great things in making our communications understandable to ordinary people.

---

1 As he was at the time he gave the address. He has subsequently become Minister of Transport.
2 This is an edited version of the speech that has been reprinted in (1995) 33 *Clarity* 11 – 15.

We are also very grateful to the British High Commission and the British Council who have helped make this seminar possible. Their country has been one of the pioneers in this area.

I have also been heartened by the enthusiasm with which both members of my own department and others have participated in this important new venture. During yesterday's all-day seminar, which dealt with topics such as legislative, drafting, guidelines for drafting in plain language, and university course material, it became clear that people are strongly committed to the idea of making our legislation and other documentation simpler and more intelligible. Many participants welcomed the initiative as something long overdue. In the legal training and education sessions, bodies involved in legal education have also demonstrated their commitment to re-examining the question of plain language in the law schools, and we are grateful to those who have come from other parts of the country to take part in our seminar. The rapporteurs from yesterday's seminar will do a short report back later this morning, but I have already been told that the seminar was stimulating, that it provoked a lot of discussion and that, in short, it made a good start to a number of projects we would like to see taking place both in and beyond the department in the very near future.

## 2  Access to justice

One of the cornerstones of our programme for the transformation of justice is the principle of people's access to justice. When tackling this question, it is hardly necessary to emphasise that many of the people in this country have had extremely negative experiences of the justice system. Many, many of our citizens have come before our courts after the trauma of a brutalising arrest and found themselves in front of a magistrate or judge who does not share their language or their culture, and who takes decisions in terms of laws which they do not understand. This is not to say that there have not been good judges or magistrates, but they too have been confined by a system which, too often, has been perceived to be in conflict with the interests of ordinary people. Because of the restricted composition of the courts, with incumbents drawn from the ranks of the privileged, the victims of that system have been alienated from the very places they should be able to look to for justice.

In addition, a legal system that defends the privileges of only one section of society can hardly lay claim to the privilege of calling itself a system of justice. This is the historical legacy with which we have to grapple.

## 3 Participatory democracy

The other key to transformation is the principle of participation. We have, at last, held proper democratic elections in this country. But we should not think that the securing of democracy is something that occurs automatically after a democratic election; something that comes about just because people vote for the government of their choice, however great that first step is.

Democracy is a goal. It is an ideal towards whose realisation we must direct all our efforts. Exercising one's rights in a democracy presupposes
- a **knowledge** and **understanding** of those rights;
- a knowledge and understanding of **how** those rights can be exercised; and
- a **capacity** to **exercise** them.

An absence of such knowledge and understanding disempowers individuals and groups. And unless the people as a whole are empowered, democracy becomes a tool in the hands of the rich and powerful. Such a situation results in alienation. People lose faith in democracy and society tends to develop greater tensions and polarisation.

That is why I call democracy an ideal. No society achieves perfect democracy, but it is and must be our obligation to achieve the very best we can in an imperfect world.

So what is it that we should be doing to ensure that we work towards this goal?

The best defenders of the rights of the people are the people themselves. I believe therefore that, if our system of justice is to serve the people of this country, we must give our citizens the means to use their rights for the benefit of themselves and their communities. We must create a culture of human rights that gives South Africans both the confidence and an internalised understanding of their rights and role in society. This is part of empowerment.

It is in the pursuit of this goal that the nature and style of public information becomes so critical. If we write laws in complicated and difficult language, how can we possibly expect the citizens of this country to understand or obey those laws? How can we expect them to use those laws for the protection of themselves and their communities? If we produce documents that are complex and inaccessible, how can we expect people to understand their rights and put them to good use?

This issue does not only apply to legislation. It goes right across the gamut of government documentation. If pamphlets and information documents and White Papers are written in language that is not understood, people cannot reasonably be expected to exercise their rights or obligations. If people cannot understand the forms they need to fill in, they may be deprived of benefits to which they are entitled. According to the Black Sash, 21 per cent of the people applying to their offices are looking for help in the filling out of government forms. And the results are clear. I will give you just one example. In respect of maintenance grants, only 24 per cent of so-called "illegitimate" coloured children receive benefits. And, according to the latest available figures, only a shocking 0,3 per cent of African children receive the grants they are entitled to.

Clear, simple, understandable communication is a whole lot more than just something we should be dreaming about. It is an absolute and critical necessity for democracy. People have a right to understand the laws that govern them, to understand court proceedings in matters that affect them, to understand what government is doing in their name.

What I am saying is that the right to information which forms part of our Bill of Rights means that people have a right to information that empowers them and their communities. They have a right to information that they can use in practical ways to make a difference to their lives.

Simplicity of language reflects a commitment to democracy. The use of language above the heads of the average citizen may swell the heads of its users, but it does little else.

Having said this, we need to look at practical ways in which we can make sure that this right to information begins to work. In this regard, there are two important issues I wish to raise.

## 4   Multilingual society

The first relates to the fact that the people of this country speak not one or two but eleven and more languages. Some of these languages have highly developed written forms and some do not. Some are spoken widely and some only in certain areas by a relatively small number of people. All of these different language speakers have an equal right to information. And I would like to say in this regard that simply translating what is obscurely written in English or Afrikaans into equally obscure Xhosa or Zulu is not the answer. We do not need eleven versions of gobbledegook. Any translator into an African language will tell you how she or he struggles with English that is written in a complicated and jargonistic way. So, whichever of our eleven languages we use, the principle remains the same. Communication should be clear, simple and understandable.

## 5    Literacy

The second point relates to the level of literacy. As we all know, one of the terrible legacies of the past is the inability of many of our citizens to read or write. This is a matter for great shame, as well as being a source of grave disempowerment.

I want to make this point strongly, because often it is neglected or forgotten. People who cannot read or write have an equal right to information and it is up to us, both in government and in civil society, acting in partnership, to make sure that they get it. And this applies equally to people who are blind, deaf or face other difficulties in accessing information. Every one of our citizens has an equal right to information and we share a responsibility to make sure each person gets the information he or she needs.

We should not, therefore, fool ourselves into thinking that if we produce a booklet or a pamphlet that is plainly written our job is done. We should be looking at additional and different ways of presenting clear and understandable information to people; ways that ensure that, at the end of the day, people have in their possession information that they can use to improve and control their lives. If information is indeed power, that is the kind of power we should be giving to people.

So you see that plain, simple and understandable language must not be confined to written language. It must inform everything we do: our radio and television broadcasts; the way we speak to people. We need to understand that this is our obligation as a service provider both as a responsible government and as organs of civil society. We must, in short, democratise language.

This does not mean, as some fear, that such an approach will interfere with literature or poetry, or that it will intervene where people of the same profession speak to one another in whatever shorthand they have developed for the purpose. It simply means that, where we communicate with the public, we must do so in a way that the public understands and can use.

## 6   Conclusion

Developing a human rights culture will depend on many things. It will depend on the full transformation of the justice system to a system that is accessible, participatory and representative of all the people of our country. It will mean that the courts should not be places of terror and alienation, but places where people can go, and believe they can go, to see and experience justice. It will mean that people and communities in fear or danger know who to approach and how to use their rights to protect themselves. It will mean that, when ordinary people are victimised for whatever reason, they know where to go for help.

But, in order to make these things happen, people must know and understand their rights. They must receive information which tells them what to do and how to do it. And they must have an internalised sense of themselves as citizens living in a democracy with rights that they can exercise and obligations they must meet. And they must know, ultimately, that justice will be done.

Only when people feel that democracy is theirs and for real, will they be prepared to defend it.

This is why I have laid such a heavy emphasis on the right to information in the Department of Justice and why we hope, in the near future, to be engaged in many communication projects designed to inform the citizens of our country about human rights, the justice system, as well as people's rights and obligations as citizens.

But whatever we do, and whatever medium or language we use, the challenge before us is to make sure that all our communications are written and spoken in a way that people can understand, a way that empowers them by giving them the information they need to take charge of their lives and exercise their rights as citizens of this country.

## D.2
# Plain language in the drafting of the 1996 Constitution

**Johann van der Westhuizen**
*Judge of the High Court, Pretoria*

> 1 Introduction ... *page 61*
> 2 The language of lawyers ... *page 62*
> 3 Constitutional drafting ... *page 63*
> 4 Mechanisms and techniques ... *page 65*
> 5 Examples ... *page 66*
> 6 Conclusion ... *page 70*

## 1   Introduction

I have been asked to speak briefly about the 1996 Constitution and other examples of innovative drafting.

Before talking about the Constitution, I wish to make a few very brief remarks about legal language in general. Thereafter I shall say something about a constitution as an instrument of empowerment, or a tool of education, or as it is sometimes referred to, the autobiography of a nation, or the window to a nation's soul. I shall speak about the decision of the Constitutional Assembly to try to use plain language as far as the 1996 Constitution is concerned, and the mechanism and the techniques used at the time, referring to a few examples of attempts at plain language. I shall also refer to some problems experienced during the process of drafting, especially as far as the interaction with the political processes is concerned.

## 2   The language of lawyers

Lawyers are notorious for the language that they use, and I cannot resist the temptation to give you an example from no less an authoritative source than the *Guinness Book of Records*. It cites the 'Nuts order' as the most incomprehensible statutory or legal provision in the English language:

> In the Nuts (underground) (other than ground nuts) Order, the expression nuts shall have reference to such nuts, other than ground nuts, as would but for this amending Order not qualify as nuts (underground) (other than ground nuts) by reason of their being nuts (underground).

Should you think this is only a joke, I will provide a constitutional example. Article 25(1)(a) of the Namibian Constitution of 1990 reads as follows:

> Save insofar as it may be authorised to do so by this Constitution, Parliament, or any subordinate legislative authority shall not make any law, and the Executive and the agencies of Government shall not take any action which abolishes or abridges the fundamental rights and freedoms conferred by this Chapter, and any law or action in contravention thereof shall to the extend of the contravention be invalid: Provided that a competent court, instead of declaring such law or action to be invalid, shall have the power and the discretion in an appropriate case to allow Parliament, any subordinate legislative authority, or the Executive and the agencies of Government, as the case may be, to correct any defect in the impugned law or action within a specified period, subject to such conditions as may be specified by it. In such event and until such correction, or until the expiry of the time limit set by the Court, whichever be the shorter, such impugned law or action shall be deemed to be valid.

I do not wish to repeat the old question: "Why do lawyers speak and write this way?" However, one must make one point very clear as far as the Constitution is concerned – the law is an important tool of social control, and language is often used as an instrument not only of communication, but certainly also of intimidation and attack.

Philosophers sometimes write that lawyers use language to obscure or distort the truth, or to find legal loopholes for their clients. That reminds me of one of the ancient Greek philosophers, Socrates, who had to appear for the first time before a people's court when he was very old. He was being charged with things such as showing disrespect to the gods and corrupting the youth of Athens. In his own defence he said to this court that the people of Athens had seen him in the market square for many years: he had always spoken to the youth of Athens in that market square; he knew nothing about the law or about technical rules. What they would hear from him was very simple language, not only because that was the only language that he knew, but also because he believed that the truth was more important than the rules and the technicalities that applied in court.

Various theories and accusations as to why lawyers write badly have been put forward. A few years ago, before I knew anything about the concept of plain language, I came across an article by Starke in the *Harvard Law Journal*. Starke concluded his article (after giving many examples) by saying that we all think that lawyers write so badly because they cannot write any better, because they are so conservative, or because they are so clumsy. But perhaps they write so badly intentionally, because it is their very job to try to confuse people. Half the time they should know that they do not have a case, and the best they can do about it is to create as much confusion as possible. Over a long period of time lawyers became used to using language as an instrument of deception. Linked to this is the issue of professional self-preservation. Lawyers speak that way because they do not want others to think that what they do for a living is easy. Otherwise clients would not see the need to pay for a lawyer's services. They would rather handle their affairs themselves.

My response to this is that it is possibly true, but don't we all do it? I find the same tendency in my doctor, my plumber and the mechanic who has to explain to me what is wrong with my car and why I have to pay him R7 000 when I thought the service would cost me R300.

## 3  Constitutional drafting

I was involved in drafting the 1996 (or Final) Constitution (Act 108 of 1996), as a member of the so-called "Panel of Constitutional Experts" advising the Constitutional Assembly in Cape Town. I was also a member of a smaller panel, which was then referred to as the "Technical Refinement Team", specifically responsible for the linguistic refinement of the draft constitutional text.

A constitution, in particular, should not read like the Nuts order. Even if we are satisfied with the idea that laws and contracts are written in that way, a constitution should not be. We like to say to one other that we have adopted a new culture of human rights and constitutionalism. It is said that a constitution is an instrument of empowerment. It tells people what their rights are, how the President is elected, who makes the laws for the country, and what the army and the police are supposed to be doing. It is an instrument of education. We want to see the Constitution, or parts of it, on posters on the walls of primary school classrooms, or police offices, or prisons. We also say to one another that we want the Constitution to be a living constitution that is cherished in the hearts and minds of people.

Also, especially in view of our history, we want the Constitution to bring about equality between people; not only equality between people of different races, but also between people of different classes: powerful people and weak people, rich people and poor people, well-educated people and people who have not had the benefit of a proper education. If all these things are true, we cannot write a constitution that reads like the Nuts order. In the years immediately preceding the Constitution, it became almost a cliché to say that a constitution is also the autobiography of a nation or the window to the soul of the nation.

If all these things are vaguely true, then a constitution must at least be a little more easily understandable to ordinary people than some of the other legislative provisions that we are talking about. To this end the Constitutional Assembly (the body that in terms of the Interim Constitution of 1993 drafted the Final Constitution) took a formal decision in 1995 that the Constitution must as far as possible be drafted in plain or simple language. At the time this decision was taken, there was generally a very clear agreement and desire that this must be done, but nobody knew exactly how this was going to happen. Drafting the Constitution in simple language was not supposed to be done by a few lawyers sitting in an office, with a minister briefing them. The drafting of a constitution is a very dynamic, and sometimes very emotional, political process, where every clause is negotiated. So, should one immediately try to draft it in plain language or should one let people talk and draft and at the end of it all hire an expert to rewrite the whole thing in plain language?

## 4  Mechanisms and techniques

The Constitutional Assembly consisted of all the members of the National Assembly and the Senate; 400 people at the time. There is no way that 400 people can draft anything. They were divided into a number of theme committees. One theme committee worked specifically on the Bill of Rights, which is Chapter 2 of the Constitution. Another theme committee worked with Parliament and the Executive, another with the police and other security services, another with the chapter on finance, and so on. Even these theme committees consisted of about 40 to 50 people each. Each theme committee was assisted by two, three or four so-called technical experts. These were academics, lawyers and other experts. The idea was that these different theme committees would negotiate, discuss and then draft sections of the Constitution. These sections were then referred to the Constitutional Committee, a committee of the Constitutional Assembly. Once again, the Constitutional Committee consisted of between 40 and 50 people.

Later in 1995 it became clear to the Constitutional Assembly that there was a serious need to publish a draft of some kind. It was then decided to appoint the Technical Refinement Team. This team consisted of a Canadian plain language expert who had earlier been involved in the drafting of the South African labour legislation. He made a presentation to the Constitutional Assembly that included many telling examples. The Constitutional Assembly liked the idea. Also included in the team were two members of our panel of experts and a very experienced drafter from the Department of Justice, who was very skilled, but also steeped in the way that legislation had been drafted up to that point. The team was chaired or convened by the Executive Director or Deputy Executive Director of the Constitutional Assembly.

The Technical Refinement Team was not at all supposed to take any decisions on substance. We were only supposed to put together all the different pieces that originated from the different theme committees. The biggest task was simply to try to make these pieces coherent and to fit them into some pattern. Sometimes much of what the theme committees had been doing up to then, with the help of all their experts, had to be rewritten entirely. A draft was then produced and circulated to the public.

During April 1996 and the first few days of May 1996 it all became very heated and hectic. The adoption date was 9 May 1996. The political debate with negotiations, thorny issues and deadlocks had been going on, but final decisions and formulations were often postponed. Texts were floating around for months with little open spaces or footnotes saying that the negotiators would return to an issue which had been flagged. A week or two before the adoption people had to make up their minds. The text required the political process of agreement, plus the drafting, and to avoid inconsistencies the drafting had to be done in such a way that it fitted in with the rest of the draft. During the last few days and hours, it was very difficult to adhere to any kind of firm plain language approach, simply because the political dynamics would not allow for it. I return to this point.

## 5   Examples

I wish to mention a few small and very obvious examples. One of the most obvious features of the 1996 Constitution, compared with the Interim Constitution, or any other previous South African legal text, is that the word "shall" is not used. Lawyers like to use "shall": Lawyers say "The president **shall** dissolve parliament"; "Everyone **shall** have the right to life"; and so on. Language experts tell us that there could be something like six different meanings for the word "shall". It could for example be a promise, or it could refer to the future, or to the present. The idea was to get rid of the word "shall". At times I was not entirely certain that this was an absolutely good idea, because sometimes the word "shall" captures a little bit of a majestic meaning which one cannot necessarily capture with other words. But be that as it may, the word "shall" was not used. Instead of saying for example "Every person shall have the right to life", the Constitution simply says "Everyone has the right to life". Is that what we want to say, that everyone has the right to life anyway, or do we want to say that one day when things are better, when democracy and human rights prevail, everyone shall have the right, or perhaps that everyone ought to have the right, even though it is not necessarily the case at present?

> **Interim Constitution** (section 10): Every person shall have the right to respect for and protection of his or her dignity.
>
> **Final Constitution** (section 10): Everyone has inherent dignity and the right to have their dignity respected and protected.

Instead of "The President shall dissolve Parliament", "The President **must** dissolve Parliament" is used. If there is no discretion, if the Constitution says that when something happens, or is at hand, the President has to do something, then the President must do it, so why not say it directly? There was some resistance even amongst ourselves, because all of a sudden it almost sounded disrespectful when you say that the President **must** now do this or that. To say that he **shall** do it, could still sound like you are saying that he is going to do it anyway, because it is the right thing, but now you say very directly that he **must**, whether he likes it or not. If there is something that the President cannot do, instead of saying "shall not", "may not" is now used. If he has a discretion, you would say that the President "may". If the President has the discretion to dissolve Parliament or not dissolve it, the word would be "may dissolve".

I find it interesting that people often think that the words "may not" also allow for discretion. If you say "When 10 people vote against it, the President may not ...", it means that he may not, "hy mag nie", in Afrikaans, he is not allowed to. But some people seem to read it as saying he may not do it or he may indeed do it; it is within his discretion. We thought that "may do it" and "may not do it" are much clearer than the "shall" and "shall not".

> **Interim Constitution** (section 12): No person shall be subject to servitude or forced labour.
>
> **Final Constitution** (section 13): No one may be subjected to slavery, servitude or forced labour.

Should you say that "the courts shall be independent and impartial" or that "the courts are independent and impartial"? What happens if, at the time that you are writing, you are not sure whether the courts are independent and impartial? On the other hand, it could be argued of course that you should say that "the courts are independent and impartial", because that is a constitutional imperative and even if they are not impartial and independent in practice, they have to be. Previous texts would have said that "the courts shall be independent and impartial and no one shall interfere with their functioning."

In the Bill of Rights, Chapter 2, it is simply stated that "everyone" has certain rights. The previous term was "every person". If you look through a window and see something happening on the street, like a carnival, you are not going to say to your colleague "Look, every person is wearing a hat", but simply "Everyone is wearing a hat". The reference to "every person" is a pretentious attempt of legal language to sound clinically and formally correct, perhaps even more to sound objective. But people do not speak in that way, unless an element of sarcasm or deliberate formality is involved.

> **Interim Constitution** (section 13): Every person shall have the right to his or her personal privacy, which shall include the right not to be subject to searches of his or her person, home or property, the seizure of private possessions or the violation of private communications.

> **Final Constitution** (section 14): Everyone has the right to privacy, which includes the right not to have –
> (a) their person or home searched;
> (b) their property searched;
> (c) their possessions seized;
> (d) the privacy of their communications infringed.

One of the principles of plain language is that you must be as clear and direct as possible when conveying meaning. To achieve this you should, where possible, avoid the passive. Lawyers like to talk in the passive: something must be done, a licence must be issued. This does not apply only to practising lawyers and judges; academics also like to write this way. They say that it is now time for some research to be done on this topic, that some serious thought should be given to an idea or problem. Sometimes I think that they do this to gain distance. You do not really want to say: 'We must do it'. Perhaps you do not want to sound arrogant, so instead of saying 'I think that ...', you say 'It could be argued ...'. For example, a rule stating that dogs are not allowed in a park without leashes could be problematic, as it would be difficult to figure out who it is that is addressed: merely the owner of a dog taking it for a walk? Should I be sitting in the park and see a dog running around without a leash, would I be in trouble if I do not chase the dog out of the park or catch it and put a leash on it? The active form of this command would make it much clearer exactly on whom there is an obligation to act. So, you will find very few instances where the passive voice is used in the Constitution, but I return to the issue of clarity.

> **Interim Constitution** (section 97(2)(a)): There shall be a President of the Constitutional Court, who shall, subject to section 99, be appointed by the President ...

**Final Constitution** (section 174(3)): The President as head of the national executive ... appoints the President ... of the Constitutional Court ...

One is always told – as we have seen from the examples that I have cited – to avoid long and clumsy sentences. However, short sentences are not necessarily clearer. Sometimes one harms the expression of a thought by breaking it into smaller sentences.

We also attempted to avoid formal, archaic terminology and to use simple and contemporary words. This venture provided interesting examples. Lawyers and experienced drafters often resisted the idea of suspending the use of an age-old term. The argument was that a new term could cause confusion, also amongst judges, as many books and cases have over the years dealt with the meaning of the old term. All these books and cases may have been necessary because no one ever knew the exact meaning of the term, and research sometimes showed that the term remained unclear.

An attempt was also made to avoid cross-referencing as far as possible. One of the causes for confusion among ordinary people and even lawyers is that one can read nothing without having to read something else first, or alongside it. An attempt was made to avoid cross-references in the Constitution. However, one sometimes cannot do without cross-references. The challenge is to organise the material in such a way that it forms a logical narrative so that one does not have to refer back and forth. On the other hand, we also know that nobody is going to read the Constitution as if it is a novel.

The issue of cross-referencing is one of the examples pertaining to the use of plain language that proved difficult by the end of the negotiating process. The negotiations were tense and the politicians sometimes insisted on cross-references. A drafting expert said that it was not really necessary to cross-refer was told that he or she was not being asked for an opinion and had to do as instructed. One must be realistic. Sometimes the re-drafting of a clause, even an improvement on what had gone before, could cause a delicate political agreement to collapse. Sometimes something that was vague had rather not be made clear because the very reason political leaders were able to agree on it was its very vagueness, which allowed politicians to please different constituencies. In other words, sometimes there may be political sense, apart from legal sense, in leaving some questions for the courts to resolve.

Not everything is about simple words or short sentences. It is also about the organisation of the material. If you look at the Constitution, you will see that there is an attempt to arrange chapters in a certain order. The first chapter consists of the so-called founding provisions. This chapter states that South Africa is a democratic sovereign state. The second chapter is the chapter on fundamental rights. The Chair of the Constitutional Assembly often said the Bill of Rights is the soul of the Constitution. Thereafter follow chapters on Parliament, the Executive, the President, and so on, and the powers of the provinces. The Chair referred to these issues as the heart of the Constitution. These chapters are followed by a chapter on the court structure. Immediately after the chapter dealing with the court structure, other institutions that are to some extent independent, such as the Public Protector, the Human Rights Commission and the Auditor General follow. Later on one finds legal government, public administration, the security forces and finances, including a few of the definitions to be found in the Constitution.

## 6  Conclusion

Many other examples and problems could be discussed, but I conclude. The 1996 Constitution is to some extent an attempt at plainer and simpler drafting language. In some chapters this is more evident than in others. Some topics are also easier to understand than others. The practical realities of especially the last days of the process were not always conducive to consistent drafting. In a process like this there may be issues and emotions that are more relevant, at least at the time, than linguistic and even legal purity. One cannot risk the collapse of a negotiating process, and perhaps risk a civil war, for the sake of having a constitution completely free of the passive voice, or cross-references. But generally I believe that the attempt was worth it. And, in spite of predictions, I am not aware of serious confusion amongst judges or anyone else because of the language used in the Constitution.

## D.3
# Some concise guidelines to the process of drafting the new Labour Relations Act in plain language[1]

**Amanda Armstrong**
*Practising attorney, Cheadle Thompson & Haysom*

> 1  Drafting in plain language ... *page 71*
> 2  Ripple effects of drafting the Labour Relations Act in plain language ... *page 75*
> 3  Excerpts from the Labour Relations Act as illustration ... *page 76*

## 1  Drafting in plain language

The Labour Relations Act, Act 28 of 1956, was one of the first statutes to be redrafted after the first democratic elections in South Africa. The drafters considered five aspects when they drafted the new Labour Relations Act (LRA), Act 66 of 1995, in plain language:
- Overall structure of the Act
- Structure within a chapter
- Sentence structure and language
- Certainty in the voice of the legal document
- Design and layout

Each of these five aspects is now discussed briefly. Differences between the old and new LRA illustrate the "new drafting style".

---
[1] This contribution is based on a schematic presentation made by way of an overhead projector.

## 1.1 Overall structure

The following goals were borne in mind in the overall redrafting of the LRA:
- Identify purpose of legislation and identity of users of statute.
- Arrangement of chapters and parts according to users' perspective  – thematically
    – chronologically
- Detail to be given in schedules and regulations.

The drafters had to keep the users of the LRA in mind:
- Employees and their trade unions
- Employers and their employers' organisations
- Department of Labour
- Dispute resolution institutions

**Structure of the old LRA:**
- Definitions
- Applications of Act
- NMC and registrars
- Registration of trade unions and employers' organisations
- Industrial Court
- Industrial boards
- Conciliation boards
- Interim relief in unfair labour practice disputes
- Mediation
- Arbitration
- Enforcement of agreements
- Effect of arbitration awards
- Exemptions and exclusions
- Various sections dealing with agreements and awards
- Records to be kept by employers
- Inspectors
- Agents of industrial councils
- Labour brokers
- Questions of law
- Prohibition of strikes or lockouts
- Victimisation
- Secrecy
- Inspection of documents
- Publication by Minister of Labour
- Assumption by Minister of Labour of functions of local authority
- Alleged partnerships
- Evidence

- Demarcation
- Determinations relating to labour brokers
- Freedom of associations
- Indemnification against losses suffered in strike or lockout
- Federations
- Regulations
- Penalties
- Prohibited employment
- Various concluding sections

The problems with the structure of the old LRA were the following:
- No table of contents
- No chapters
- Not drafted from users' perspective
- Provisions not arranged thematically
- Provisions not arranged chronologically
- No use of schedules

**Structure of the new LRA**
- Chapter I: Purpose, application and interpretation
- Chapter II: Freedom of associations and general protections
- Chapter III: Collective bargaining
  - Part A: Organisational rights
  - Part B: Collective agreements
  - Part C: Bargaining councils
  - Part D: Bargaining councils in public service
  - Part E: Statutory councils
  - Part F: General provisions concerning councils
- Chapter IV: Strikes and lockouts
- Chapter V: Workplace forums
- Chapter VI: Trade unions and employers' organisations
  - Part A: Registration and regulation of trade unions and employers' organisations
  - Part B: Regulation of federations
  - Part C: Registrar of labour relations
  - Part D: Appeals from registrar's decision
- Chapter VII: Dispute resolution
  - Part A: Commision for Conciliation, Mediation and Arbitration (CCMA)
  - Part B: Accreditation
  - Part C: Resolution of disputes by CCMA
  - Part D: Labour Court
  - Part E: Labour Appeal Court
  - Part F: General provisions applicable to courts established by Act

- Chapter VIII: Unfair dismissal
- Chapter IX: General provisions
- Schedule 1: Establishment of bargaining councils for public service
- Schedule 2: Guidelines for construction of workplace forum
- Schedule 3: CCMA
- Schedule 4: Dispute resolution flow diagrams
- Schedule 5: Amendment of laws
- Schedule 6: Laws repealed
- Schedule 7: Transitional arrangements
- Schedule 8: Code of good practice for dismissals

## 1.2  Structure within a chapter

With respect to structure within a chapter, the following guidelines were used:
- Put more important issues at beginning
- Consider likely chronology of events
- Deal with basic principles before detail
- Move from known information to new information
- Deal with general provisions before conditions and exceptions
- Keep sections, subsections and paragraphs short
- Have one sentence for each concept

## 1.3  Sentence structure and language

The following tenets of the plain language approach were applied:
- Use short well-constructed sentences (subject – verb – object)
- Use active rather than passive voice
- Be positive
- Avoid "clause sandwiches" for example subject-clause-predicate
- Use clear and simple language
- Avoid unnecessary words and details
- Use gender-neutral language
- Minimise cross-references

## 1.4 Certainty of the voice of the legal document

To ensure that the voice of the Act is certain, the following principles were applied:
- Mandatory – use "must" to impose a duty
  (See for example section 191(3) of the new LRA below.)
- Permissive – use "may" to confer a power
  (See for example section 191(2) of the new LRA below.)
- Prohibitive – use "may not" to forbid an action
- Declaratory – use verb "to be" to state a fact

## 1.5 Design and layout

To improve the design and layout, the following design tools were used:
- Document must be user-friendly and attractive
- Provide a table of contents
- Divide document into chapters and schedules
- Divide chapters into parts, sections, subsections and paragraphs
- Use headings
- Use page-headers
- Identify defined terms (by using italics)
- Supply footnotes
- Use flow diagrams, tables and other graphic tools to illustrate relevant points
- Text must be adequately spaced
- Typeface must be legible

## 2 Ripple effects of drafting the Labour Relations Act in plain language

Drafting the LRA in plain language has led to the following documents also being drafted in plain language:
- Regulations were also drafted in plain language.
- CCMA forms have been drafted in plain language.
- Department of Labour's *Guide to the new LRA* has been drafted in plain language.
- Department's newspaper supplement *Know your LRA* has been drafted in plain language.

- Constitutions of councils were drafted in plain language.
- Collective agreements were drafted in plain language.
- CCMA commissioners are now being trained to draft awards in plain language,
- And Labour Court judges are being trained to draft decisions in plain language.

## 3    Excerpts from the Labour Relations Act as illustration

LABOUR RELATIONS ACT, 1995 – Act No 66, 1995
Unfair Dismissal
S191

>   *(c)* if an employer refused to reinstate or re-employ the *employee*, the date of *dismissal* is the date on which the employer first refused to reinstate or re-employ that *employee*.
>
>   **191.    Disputes about unfair dismissals**[52]
>
>   (1) If there is a *dispute* about the fairness of a *dismissal*, the dismissed *employee* may refer the *dispute* in writing within 30 days of the date of *dismissal* to –
>   *(a)* a *council*, if the parties to the *dispute* fall within the *registered scope* of that *council*; or
>   *(b)* the Commission, if no *council* has jurisdiction.
>
>   (2) If the *employee* shows good cause at any time, the *council* or the Commission may permit the *employee* to refer the *dispute* after the 30-day time limit has expired.
>
>   (3) The *employee* must satisfy the *council* or the Commission that a copy of the referral has been *served* on the employer.
>
>   (4) The *council* or the Commission must attempt to resolve the *dispute* through conciliation.
>
>   (5) If a *council* or a commissioner has certified that the *dispute* remains unresolved, or if 30 days have expired since the *council* or the Commission received the referral and the *dispute* remains unresolved –

---

[52] See flow diagrams Nos 10, 11, 12 and 13 in Schedule 4.

## FLOW DIAGRAM 12

### UNFAIR DISMISSAL (3)
### (Misconduct / Incapacity)

Chapter VIII (section 191)

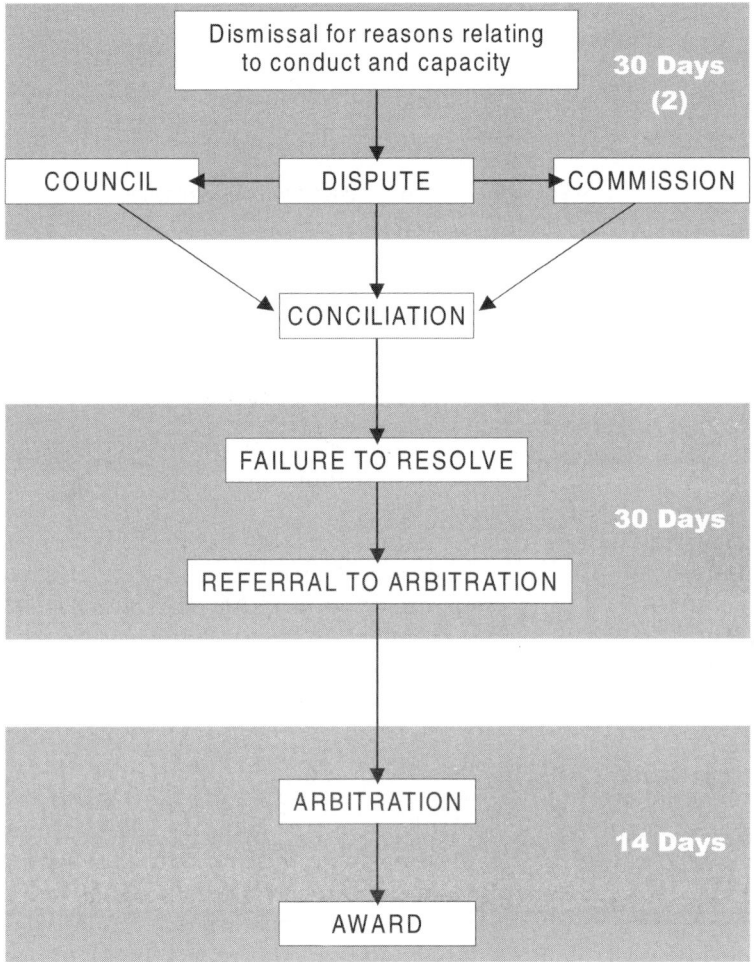

1. Dismissal for misconduct and incapacity is dealt with in the Code of Good Practice: Dismissal in Schedule 8.
2. The time limit is designed to ensure that disputes are dealt with as soon as possible. Condonation can be granted if there is good cause to do so.

## D.4
# Plain language in the current practice of drafting

**Enver Daniels**
*Chief State Law Adviser*

---

1 Introduction ... *page 78*
2 Process of transformation ... *page 80*
3 My approach to plain language ... *page 81*
4 Legislative process ... *page 83*
5 Development of clarity guidelines ... *page 83*
6 Conclusion ... *page 85*

---

## 1    Introduction

This conference on plain language is very important, because it is intended to consider the very way in which we communicate complex issues to people.

Language is a form of communication, but not the only form of communication. People need to communicate with one another in various ways, for various reasons and under different circumstances. Parliament is an instrument of change and is at the forefront of transformation. It needs to reflect that role at all times, in different ways. For example, there are a number of persons who are paralysed. To communicate with others they need assistance. One Member of Parliament is deaf. Two persons assist her by translating what is said using sign language. Two people are blind and two are partially sighted. Parliament has taken measures to ensure that they fulfil their roles as parliamentarians fully. I have specifically mentioned Parliament, because it has taken a lead in ensuring that political parties are able to nominate any person, irrespective of such a person's disability to represent them and the electorate. Facilities have been made available to ensure that such public representatives are able to communicate fully with other parliamentarians and the electorate.

In the 19th century boats were at greater risk than they are today. Shipbuilders had not yet acquired all the technology that is available today to make shipping safer. Boats were particularly at risk because of an inability to communicate with land or with other ships. That improved considerably when in 1872 Samuel Morse devised his code in which letters of the alphabet are represented by long or short light or sound signals. In the context of its time, it was an invention of great significance, although it has perhaps only limited use today. The great speed at which things move today, probably hastened this development. Imagine, for example, an aircraft flying at 900 km/h using Morse code to request permission to land. Developments in the field of aeronautics, shipping, aviation, war and even motor manufacturing, amongst other things, have necessitated faster, more efficient forms of communication. The greatest impetus to this development has probably come from globalisation. The need to facilitate trade, financial transactions and other forms of commerce requires swift communications – so swift in fact that capital can be moved through different time zones at any time, many times a day, before people have even woken up.

It is in this context that we need to examine the concept of plain language today. What we do know is that for communications to be properly understood, they need to be as plain or as simple as possible, even in this super technological world of ours. If the need to communicate efficiently by radio, satellite or computer requires the messages to be clear and simple, then communications with ordinary people in respect of daily transactions and for various other reasons, which I shall attempt to look at, need to be as plain as possible. This will help to empower people, instil a sense of confidence in them and avoid malpractices.

The use of plain language in legislation promotes more effective communication with those to whom the legislation is addressed. Any language, as a form of communication, is designed to concentrate on those grammatical structures and words which are readily understood. The drafting of legislation, using language as a medium, cannot attempt to be an exact science, since language is not an instrument of mathematical precision. We also need to understand this concept within our own South African context. It is a context in which inequalities, brought about by our apartheid past, still abound. The result today is high levels of illiteracy. On 29 June 1999, the Minister of Education, Prof Kader Asmal, mentioned that he hopes to eradicate illiteracy by 2004. One can only imagine what positive effects that will have on the whole of South African society.

## 2 Process of transformation

In South Africa today, we are witnessing a transformation process which is probably unlike anything else taking place anywhere in the world. The law in this country was used as an instrument of oppression and needed to be understood only by those who administered, applied and enforced it. Nobody else needed to know the contents of a law and nobody was expected to question its substance. In many respects that attitude, that could-not-care attitude, permeated South African society and probably explains why few institutions bothered to prepare documents in a way which was easily understood by ordinary people. I say this because Parliament must take the lead in keeping people fully informed about matters which affect them. For that reason, it must ensure that its legislation is drafted in easily understood language. Once Parliament fulfils its obligation in this respect fully, then the rest of society will follow.

I mentioned earlier that we are witnessing a transformation process. It is a process designed to redress the inequalities of the past, restore the rule of law and foster respect for fundamental human rights. Ordinary people need to have confidence in this process. They need to understand it, inform the process, accept it, participate in it and be enthusiastic about it. Once this happens, then we shall be well on the way to creating a normal society in which there is mutual respect for the dignity and rights of others. People will resort to the law, not violence or other illegal means to settle disputes, even domestic ones. Therefore, the use of plain language is very important. If we are serious about creating a caring society, then the laws of this country must be easily accessible and understood by all.

I am pleased to mention that some attention is being given to this. Legislation is being drafted as simply as possible. Sometimes, explanatory notes are inserted in the text. This is designed to help people to understand the legislation more easily. I should perhaps point out that these notes are not aids to the judicial interpretation of the legislation. They are for the benefit of ordinary people who may need some help to understand the legislation.

## 3 My approach to plain language

In dealing with the matter, you will notice that my approach to plain language differs in some respects from that of Martin Cutts who in his book, *The Plain Language Guide*[1] states as follows:

> I would rather describe plain English than define it. In my view, plain English refers to:
>
> > The writing and setting out of essential information in a way that gives a co-operative, motivated person a good chance of understanding the document at first reading, and in the same sense that the writer meant it to be understood.
> >
> > This means pitching the language at a level of sophistication that suits the readers and using appropriate structure and layout to help them navigate through the document. It does not mean using simple words at the expense of the most accurate words or writing whole documents in kindergarten language – even if, as some adult literacy surveys claim, some seven million adults in the UK and about seventy million adults in the US cannot read and write completely.

According to GC Thornton,[2] who is regarded internationally as the leading authority on legislative drafting, the principal purposes of legislation are:
- to **establish** and **delimit** the law; and
- to **communicate** the law from the lawmaking authority to society and particular persons affected by it.

The primary duty of a legislative drafter is to convert, into legislative form, the policy decisions of the government, that is to ensure that those decisions are framed as rules of law. Drafters also need to ensure that the policy is fully reflected or captured in the legislation. This, nevertheless, needs to be done in a way which achieves the purposes mentioned by Thornton.

A law is primarily communicated to the following groups of people:
- **Lawmakers** who must understand what they are debating and voting for
- Persons, usually **public officials,** who must administer and enforce the law
- **Persons who are personally affected** by the law (for example taxpayers)

---

1 (1995).
2 *Legislative Drafting* (4th ed), p 47.

- **Persons who advise** the persons affected by the law (for example legal practitioners, accountants and consultants)
- **Members of the judiciary** who have to interpret the law.

The style which is suitable for a particular law will to some extent depend on the class of persons affected by the law. Although many laws apply to society as a whole, most laws apply only to sections of society. It is, therefore, absurd to advocate that all laws should, or could, be drafted in a language and in a style which are instantly understood by ordinary people, although we can strive to achieve that goal. Transitional and saving provisions in legislation are by their very nature often complicated and cannot be drafted in "plain language". They might be drafted plainly, but would probably not be precise. The same applies to technical laws. Such laws would probably not be understood by most people, but are designed to accomplish something specific. If it reaches those who matter, it would have achieved its objective and may be regarded as a good law. Fundamental rights are enshrined in the Constitution together with many other provisions which stipulate how society is to function. Therefore, the constitution itself must, of necessity, be understood by everyone, particularly if we wish to promote that caring society which we speak of. Even in this regard, many problems have already arisen.

Plain language is, in many legal contexts, anything but plain. The concept suggests that there is an ideal way to say things that will suit all audiences. However, audiences differ. Therefore, it is permissible to target different focus groups and to draft legislation in ways which take those interests into account. Laws often deal with very complex issues, and the issues themselves are not open to plain statement. People will not understand the law, unless the issues are understood. I need to state, though, that people will always differ in their interpretation of the law. The danger of using "plain language" in a law in a way which accomplishes simplicity, but not precision, is that it would probably give rise to more litigation than laws which are precise, but not necessarily simple.

Every legislative drafter should pursue clarity in legislation. Clarity in this context requires simplicity **and** precision. The two concepts of simplicity and precision are of equal importance – the one should not be pursued to the detriment of the other. The demands of each concept require a compromise between the precision of technical language and the use of ordinary, simple words.

## 4 Legislative process

In South Africa, legal administration officers of the sponsoring government department, sometimes assisted by private consultants, prepare draft Bills which are, after Cabinet's approval, submitted to the State Law Advisers for certification.

During this process, the State Law Advisers ensure that the draft Bill is consistent with the Constitution and in harmony with existing statute law. The Law Advisers should also ensure that the Bill is drafted as simply and as clearly as possible. The pursuit of clarity involves consistency of style and approach. There must also be consistency in word choice and usage, and in stylistic practices (for example numbering, spelling and presentation), as well as a consistent approach to similar problems. Clarity should be sought not only in the Bill itself, but also in relation to other existing legislation. To achieve consistency is, however, time consuming.

The work of the State Law Advisers is often hampered by:
- variations in drafting styles and techniques by the respective government departments;
- pressure to certify lengthy, and often complicated, draft Bills within a short period of time; and
- reluctance of departments to accept changes to formulations, especially if those formulations are the result of consultation.

Sometimes the State Law Advisers change a draft Bill drastically, especially its form, not only for consistency, but to clarify and simplify formulations.

In order to alleviate the above problems, the possibility of submitting draft Bills to the State Law Advisers for certification *before* they are submitted to Cabinet for approval is being considered. Government departments are also encouraged to involve the State Law Advisers in the design stage of new legislation. This has enabled the State Law Advisers to play a more prominent role in the initial drafting of legislation and to ensure that its provisions are as clear and simple as possible.

## 5 Development of clarity guidelines

Currently there are no established guidelines or criteria for the use of plain language in the drafting of legislation in South Africa.

Without doubt, good legislative drafting practice in any country requires uniformity or consistency of usage among all drafters in that country. A practice manual for State Law Advisers which provides, amongst other things, clarity guidelines for legislation is currently being prepared by the State Law Advisers. It is envisaged that this manual will be finalised later this year.

The primary purpose of such clarity guidelines will be to ensure that a legislative drafter:

- writes simply but precisely;
- drafts for the audience;
- organises content logically;
- avoids long sentences without paragraphs;
- omits unnecessary or outdated words and expressions;
- uses common words, rather than elaborate or obscure ones;
- uses the active rather than the passive voice where possible; and
- as far as possible, limits the use of cross-referencing to other parts of legislation and, more particularly to other legislation.

Even though these guidelines have not been formalised, the underlying concepts of simplicity and precision are being supported and actively pursued by the State Law Advisers. The *Guidelines for Drafting in Plain English* is a manual for legislative drafters of the Law Reform Commission of Victoria (in the Commonwealth of Australia) and Thornton's rules[3] for the pursuit of clarity show that South African laws apply some of these guidelines and rules. Through legislative drafting courses, in-house training and the sharing of knowledge State Law Advisers are sensitised as to the necessity of accomplishing simplicity and precision. This applies to amendments to existing legislation as well. Our in-house training sessions are also attended by officials from the Justice Department, who are responsible for drafting legislation initiated by Justice, and officials from some other government departments. Greater consistency, clarity and simplicity in South African legislation would be achieved if such training, based on uniform standards and practices, is extended to all government departments.

In order to establish clarity guidelines for legislation the following are being considered:

---

3   pp 53 – 74.

- The views of internationally recognised drafters such as Thornton and V Crabbe[4]
- *Guidelines for Drafting in Plain English* of Victoria
- Authorities on the use of plain language in general
- Drafting issues arising from the Constitution and other legislation such as labour legislation passed since 1995 (Labour Relations, Basic Conditions of Employment, Employment Equity and Skills Development Acts), the South African Schools Act, 1996 and the National Water Act, 1998 – these laws, to some extent, deviated from the drafting style and presentation of other laws passed by Parliament and adopted some of the practices advocated by the supporters of "plain language".

If the clarity guidelines are to be applied universally, that is, in respect of national and provincial legislation, municipal by-laws and subordinate legislation, all interested parties should be consulted.

These guidelines, however, ought not to inhibit the particular style of a drafter since style is a relative matter and no absolute judgments may be passed. According to Thornton[5] no arbitrary line can be drawn between "good style" and "bad style", and the degree to which the manner of expression achieves the purposes of legislation is the sole measure of the quality of the style. The drafters who write **clearly and simply** are most likely to communicate, successfully, the purposes of legislation.

The establishing of clarity guidelines to be used in respect of all legislation would go a long way towards enhancing the clarity of legislation for its users.

## 6    Conclusion

The fact that plain language usage is likely to feature more prominently in the future is an exciting development. The law will be more accessible to ordinary people. This will achieve one of our objectives and will promote the rule of law. But its importance lies in the fact that other institutions, the banks, insurance companies, lawyers and others must inevitably follow suit. The benefits for South African society as a whole will be enormous.

---

4    See his book, *Legislative Drafting*, 1993.
5    p 46.

## D.5
# A practitioner's perspective: Leases in plain language[1]

**Chris Leppan**
*Group Legal Adviser, WesBank*

At WesBank we have concentrated on all our documentation, not just on lease agreements. In fact there are about 19 documents, including all maintenance leases, operating leases and instalment agreements. There are many of them. We have applied the same principles to all.

In 1995 I was serving on the Council of Southern African Banks and was asked by the Chairman to appear on one of these early morning TV chat shows on behalf of the banking community. Five minute before the lights went on on stage, I was under the impression that I was both an attorney and a banker – two very noble professions. But to use a rugby analogy, I have been given a horrific task. Francois Pienaar might have had the nation behind him when he won the world cup, but I promise you I could very rapidly tell that I had the nation in front of me and they were coming at me rather fast. The banking community was ripped apart, and I had to stand there and try and defend it.

What came through very strongly was that the public, basically, did not like nor trust banks. Even though there were bankers or attorneys that thought otherwise, it was very clear that we were not liked and we were not trusted. I was very fortunate because my MD had to watch the programme, which might have been a good thing or a bad thing, but the long term benefits were good as he also picked up what the public was saying. At WesBank we have what we call customer satisfaction in-depth, a customer survey. Whenever a new customer enters into a new agreement with us, we send him (or her) a short questionnaire asking what

---

1 This is only an excerpt from Chris Leppan's presentation.

he or she thought of us. With these kind of things generally you get about a 12 or 15 per cent response, but it is about the best gauge that we have. What came through very clearly was that in 1996–97 only 59 per cent of customers understood our documents. That is not really good. That means that almost 50 per cent of our customers did not know what they had signed for, they were not happy with the document.

As Legal Adviser I now had to try to help or answer questions not only from customers but especially from staff. Time and time again, people would come and ask what something meant and I would have to take them through it. At the same time, (it was a bad week) there was a big project on the go, pressure was building, and one of our young BDO's (Business Development Officers) came into my office and she needed an explanation on a contract. Sad to say, I was a little irritable, and somewhat short at the time because I had this other project on the go. She asked me what something meant. I sat back and said to her: "Well, thís is whát it méans" and I took her through it very slowly. She was also this frustrated because she had a customer that she had to deal with and she was also under pressure. She just looked at me and said "Then for heaven's sake, why didn't you write it that way?" I was somewhat shaken, but that was really what got the ball going.

So then we sat down and started trying to write our documents simply. I was very fortunate at the time as I had the support of my MD. What he wanted us to do was to gain the trust of our customers, and we wanted to gain their rust in clear and direct communication. That was the cornerstone for our whole project.

How did I go about it? To be honest, I was rather alone, because I had not come across much writing on the subject. At the time the South African Law Commission was looking into the Unfair Terms in Contracts Bill, and I attended some of their talks. What came through very clearly was the strong consumer interest. And that is what we also addressed. One of the things was, and it might seem small I know, that the print had to be in point 10. And I'll show you what point 10 is, it is a reasonable sized print, whereas all banks had been printing their documents in about point 7. And that is significantly smaller. So we said, "OK, all documents should be in point 10".

Another principle developed: no Latin. So we said, "Fine, let's get rid of the Latin." That is when it gets to be fun, because the lawyers amongst you will appreciate that since you had to start as lawyers you have come to use and accept Latin. Now you have to put that into plain language that people will understand. That is when things become fun, but we used no Latin – we did away with Latin. *Domicillium* goodbye. All that went out the window.

We then had to take it a step further. We had to ask about legal terms? Does the average man in the street understand what cession is? Does he understand what I mean when I talk of attornment? No, he does not. We have to translate it, put it into language that all could understand. We said we were writing for our customers, not for fellow attorneys or judges.

Within WesBank there are basic two sub-structures: One we call WesBank Motor which deals in normal motor vehicle finance, and the other is WesBank Corporate which handles the larger fleets, shipping, plant and equipment, and aircrafts. And we had two slightly different approaches. When I first launched the programme in the bank, I made a very silly mistake of opening an executive meeting by saying that we would be speaking plain and simple language. That was wrong. The moment I said simple, everybody turned off; they thought I was being patronising. It was a big mistake. But nevertheless, ultimately we won the day. What we had to do was that for the motor car section we used it very plain language, very plain and down to earth. On the corporate side we retained certain legal terms. The corporate people felt that they dealt with managing directors, financial directors and the like and therefore they wanted something slightly different. So we have done what I now term "not plain or simple language" but "user-friendly language."

# D.6
# Plain language in a multilingual society

### Mariëtta Alberts
*Centre for Legal Terminology in African Languages (CLTAL), Pretoria*

---

1   Introduction ... *page 89*
2   Language of law, legal language, legalese or
    "plain language"? ... *page 90*
3   Language development in a multilingual country ... *page 91*
4   The South African situation regarding multilingual
    legal terminology ... *page 92*
5   Problems relating to terminology ... *page 94*
6   Conclusion ... *page 115*
7   Bibliography ... *page 116*

---

## 1   Introduction

Terminology is a strategic resource in a multilingual country. It is the medium through which knowledge and information are disseminated. Through the use of systematically documented terminology, correct, standardised and effective scientific and technical communication skills are developed. This enables subject specialists to communicate meaningfully with one another as well as with laypersons.

When dealing with legal terminology, we not only have to deal with a multilingual society, but also with legalese: a technical language used by legal experts – and incomprehensible to laypeople. A further complication is that, although Roman Dutch Law forms the basis of the South African legal system, it is also greatly influenced by *inter alia* British Common Law and Indigenous Law. This poses a serious problem when determining the exact meaning of a concept. It is therefore necessary to excerpt legal terms from a variety of existing documentation and first of all to define these concepts accurately with regard to the South African context before it is possible to denote them with equivalents in any of the official languages. Only a term with an exact meaning that portrays the concept will promote exact communication.[1]

## 2 Language of law, legal language, legalese or "plain language"?

Complex knowledge in a variety of sub-languages is transferred through specialised language usage (called Language for Special Purposes (LSP) or terminology). In cases where texts from specialised domains acquire the status of public documents, the information needs to be transferred into a less formal register. In the case of legal documents, such as insurance policies, civil codes and other written instruments of the law to which the broad public has access, there has been a movement towards the use of "plain language".[2]

Legal terminology is an appropriate vehicle for the formalisation of legal knowledge. Lawyers have formed definite concepts for human beings, objects, and processes through abstraction and logical thinking. Traditionally, this knowledge is represented in definitions in acts, judgements or literature. Legal information systems communicate in written language through text documents.[3]

Historical, sociological, political and jurisprudential factors have contributed to the unique characteristics of legal language.[4] Legal language has an important role in regulating society and therefore society has a right to demand more comprehensible legal language.

Advocates for the simplification of legal language argue that most complicated legal pronouncements have simpler and more easily understood equivalents in ordinary English and that plain legal language would serve both the lawyers and law students as well as the general public.[5]

These arguments are countered by those who defend legal language as being more precise, actually shorter and more durable

---

1    Alberts (1997a) 1.
2    Kittredge & Lehrberger (1982) 5.
3    Schweighofer & Scheithauer (1996) 59.
4    Charrow, Crandall & Charrow (1982) 178–188.
5    Sambo (1997) 27.

and intelligible than everyday English. This orientation of linguistic usage within the law toward legal institutions rather than toward the public is probably one of the most basic reasons why its special form appears to have been preserved.[6]

There are some dimensions of legal language which have impeded comprehension on the part of the non-specialised users (laypeople). A number of factors, including social ones, have made it difficult to modernise or otherwise simplify some of the most marked features of legal terminology. The sociolinguistic factors involved in standardising professional terminology, which tends to be very formal, are bound to become more and more important. This is, especially so as the movement towards democratising specialised areas of knowledge is faced with the growing sub-specialisation and professionalisation of the increasingly complex subject matter.[7]

Many legal experts are aware of the difficulties that laypeople have in understanding legal discourse, but they tend to attribute these difficulties to a combination of esoteric vocabulary and the conceptual complexity of the law.[8]

## 3    Language development in a multilingual country

Now, what do we do with legal language in a multilingual society? Although English is taking centre stage as the *lingua franca*, there is a definite move towards multilingualism in our country. The contact between various language groups necessitates multilingual terminology lists or dictionaries.

In its report *Towards a National Language Plan for South Africa*, the Language Plan Task Group (Langtag) states that the adoption of a multilingual approach to public affairs obviously implies the use of African languages in the legal sphere as well.[9]

The role of language in development cannot be overemphasised. Language is the vehicle for the transmission of scientific and technical information and it is the vehicle and manifestation of culture.[10] Languages can be empowered to be potent media of development. It is a given that information is assimilated best

---

6   Sambo (1997) 27.
7   Kittredge & Lehrberger (1982) 5.
8   Charrow & Charrow 1975, 1976;  Charrow, Crandall & Charrow (1982) 176.
9   Cf Langtag (1995) Sambo (1997) 27.
10  Cf Bamgbose (1991) Oyetade (1998) 39.

through the mother tongue. Research has shown that orthographical differences are relatively immaterial.[11] Too many linguistic forms can, however, hamper the assimilation of information and there is a need for language standardisation and for the harmonisation of related languages.

Political and societal changes have largely transformed the functional role of the indigenous languages. In the new democratic South Africa, the Constitution provides for multilingualism and the development of the linguistic heritage. A substantial demand for terminology creation has arisen from this since various business matters (civil service departments, local administrative bodies, courts of law, among others) are now being conducted in the vernacular.[12]

Multilingualism in South Africa is a sociolinguistic fact that has to be taken seriously.[13] A large proportion of the indigenous population of South Africa can be reached only by means of indigenous languages. Information flow is hampered from being established by factors such as low literacy rates and terminologically poorly developed African languages.[14]

## 4 The South African situation regarding multilingual legal terminology

What do we do in South Africa? In a developing society such as ours there are great demands for the indigenous languages to be used at a higher level for technical and scientific communication. It has been realised that the legal profession also needs to cope with a variety of situations where there is a dire need for multilingual legal terminology.

At the annual general meeting of the South African Translators' Institute (SATI) in 1985, translators, interpreters and other officials from various government departments in South Africa indicated that they were encountering numerous problems with legal terminology when translating legal documents, compiling legislation and interpreting in court, since legal terminology in the African languages either did not exist or was inadequate.

---

11  Cf Oyetade (1998) 38.
12  Cf Mtintsilana and Morris (1988) 109.
13  Alberts (1998) 230.
14  Fourie (1994) 132.

SATI then requested the erstwhile National Terminology Services of the Department of National Education[15] to investigate the situation. The consultation and needs assessment survey indicated a need for terminology in criminal law and related sub-fields as the domains of greatest priority.

A working group was formed in 1987 and became the Committee for Legal Terminology in African Languages. Since 1996 this committee has been known as the Centre for Legal Terminology in African Languages (CLTAL). It comprises representatives from different relevant disciplines and all members are voluntary workers.

The first programme or focal area concerned the terminology for criminal law, criminal procedure and law of evidence. An extensive terminology database has been established and acceptable definitions to facilitate the proper understanding of the concepts underlying the terms have been supplied by researchers and terminologists. Legal experts are constantly verifying the database.

Because the Sepedi speakers were the first to draw attention to the deficiencies mentioned, Sepedi (Northern Sotho) was chosen as the first African language into which terms would be translated. The CLTAL also plans terminology lists for the other official South African languages. Any interested language group is most welcome to use the CLTAL as the umbrella organisation when working on criminal law, criminal procedure and law of evidence in any of the other official languages. The CLTAL will make the data already collected available to other language groups. There is, for instance, already data available in Siswati and Sesotho. A Sesotho committee was established during 1998 in the Free State to continue with the Sesotho legal terminology project. An urgent attempt will be made during 1999 to start with a proper Nguni project and to establish a committee to make their much needed contributions to this project.

The Centre encountered interesting problems while working on the first part of the above programme because of the various legal systems (Roman Dutch Law, British Common Law and Indigenous Law) applicable in South Africa. It was very difficult to unite these principles and procedures. The CLTAL soon discovered that it was vital to write definitions to explain the legal concepts. It was equally important to ensure exact communication by retaining the legal meaning. A further problem facing the project

---

15  Now the Division for Terminology and Place Names (T&PN) of the National Language Service (NLS) of the Department of Arts, Culture, Science and Technology (DACST).

team was that there were no explanatory legal dictionaries on the South African legal system available for purposes of research. The Centre had to ensure that the definitions would be acceptable to the legal professions, yet simple enough to be understood by people at grassroots level. If not, these laws and procedures would give rise to controversy.

The CLTAL is about to publish its first *Trilingual Dictionary of Criminal Law, Criminal Procedure and Law of Evidence,* which contains Sepedi and Afrikaans equivalents and definitions of defined English terms. In the next phase of the current programme, mothertongue subject specialists will supply term equivalents in the other official languages. The target group for which this terminology is intended includes legal practitioners, interpreters, translators, compilers of legislation, students of law, and even the man in the street.

The CLTAL would like to start the next stage in providing legal terms in the African languages. The compilation of a technical dictionary is a major task that requires a lot of time and dedication. Terminology work should therefore be needs driven. The CLTAL distributed a needs assessment questionnaire in January 1999 to consult subject specialists, linguists, language workers and mothertongue speakers on the feasibility of a multilingual dictionary in other domains of the legal spectrum.

The members of the Centre are looking forward to co-operating with the existing and the envisaged national lexicography units (NLUs). It also intends collaborating with the provincial language committees and with the envisaged language bodies to be established by the Pan-South African Language Board (PANSALB).

## 5    Problems relating to terminology

### 5.1    Word formation principles

Language is one of the tools used in the communication process. Exact communication can only be achieved if the sender of the message and the receiver thereof attach the same meaning to the given message. Ambiguity gives rise to confusion and distortion of the communication process. One way to ascertain the exact meaning of a message conveyed through the medium of language is to standardise the language. That is precisely what terminology is all about. It is the task of the terminologist to make sure that basic terminology principles and language attitudes are taken into account when denoting concepts and coining terms.

### 5.1.1 Interrelationship between concept and term

A term is created when various linguistic labels are used to describe or name a specific object or concept. There is a special interrelationship between the symbol, the concept (that is the mental representation thereof in one's mind) and the various linguistic labels used in different languages to describe the object or concept.

Terminology has at least three dimensions:
- Cognitive, which relates the linguistic forms to their conceptual content, that is the references in the real world
- Linguistic, which examines the existing and potential forms of the representation of terminologies (specialised domains as well as orthographies of source and target languages)
- Communicative that looks at the use of terminologies, and especially at the standardisation processes.

When everyone in a specific language group understands the same by a specific concept denoted by the specific linguistic labels, one can consider the term to be standardised. This model can be represented schematically as follows:

| Concept | Symbol | Linguistic representation in different languages |
|---------|--------|--------------------------------------------------|
| ● | 1 | one / een / uno / eins / tee / nngwe / nngwe / inye / ukunye |
| ●● | 2 | two / twee / duo / zwei / pedi / pedi / bobedi / isibini / isibili |

According to this diagram there are several cases where the transliterated forms show unified structures in related languages.

International communication (and for that matter national communication) is impeded when corresponding concepts do not coincide, and when the system of naming of concepts differs from language to language. Hence it can be argued that these difficulties can be overcome by the agreement of concepts and systems of concepts, that is when the concepts and systems of concepts are standardised.

In so far as legal systems are compatible in principle, it is also possible to standardise the terminology associated with the legal systems. If a concept does not exist in the legal system of a specific language group, it is very difficult to denote it in that language. Problems were for instance encountered when the concept "high treason" had to be given a Sepedi equivalent, because the concept is foreign to the speech community.

Variation of terminology is possible in peripheral or related disciplines (like Psychology and Sociology) or languages (eg difference between billion in English/German – American English/ French) where the same term is used for different concepts. This leads to confusion in interdisciplinary communication and the coined terms cannot penetrate.

| Concept | English/German | American English/French |
|---------|----------------|--------------------------|
| $10^9$  | milliard       | **billion**              |
| $10^{12}$ | **billion**  | trillion                 |

A concept with its unique term, therefore, has to be standardised to ensure exact communication. The terminologist standardises concepts and their related terms by defining the concepts. Exact communication is only possible when there is a one-to-one relation between term and concept. The relationship is established by means of a definition. This can be illustrated with the terms **arsonist** and **pyromaniac**. Both these terms describe a person who sets fire to an object, but there is a huge difference between them:
- An **arsonist** is a criminal who deliberately sets fire to something, especially a building.
- A **pyromaniac** is a person who cannot control the desire to set fire to things, often because of mental illness.

### 5.1.2 Culture-specific nature of terms

Owing to the culture-specific nature of some terms they cannot always be translated successfully by different cultural groups. Although to the layperson it may seem that all concepts are represented in all languages, this is definitely not the case and speakers/translators/terminologists experience great difficulty if the national and cultural backgrounds of the source and target languages differ from one another. The terminologist that tries to supply source language terminology with target language terminology without considering the cultural and ideological differences between source and target languages may possibly alter the original meaning of the concept. It is also possible that a specific language group may use the **same term** (that is linguistic symbol) to denote **different concepts** as in the case of **blue/green** in the African languages.

Concept   Linguistic representation in different languages

**blue**   blue / blou / *botala* / *-tala*, putswa / *-tala* / *-luhlaza* / *-luhlaza*; -zulucwathile

**green**   green / groen / *tala* / *botala* / *tala* / uhlaza / *luhlaza*

Confusion is created when a concept is named by different symbols in a given language. The resemblance in the equivalents of **blue/green** in the African languages is an example of how these unified forms can lead to confusion.

A person working on a multilingual legal terminology project must have a sound background of legal approach and court procedure coupled with a good command of Afrikaans and/or English and the vernacular of the relevant language groups. It is important to realise that the terminology list or dictionary will be the channel through which legal and linguistic information will flow. This terminology list or dictionary should also contain extra information on usage. It should not only be a glossary of legal terms, but should guide the user on language and style usage, on the difference in interpreting and translating certain concepts, and on misinterpreting, misstating and mispresenting.

Culture plays an important role in the translation of terms. The translated equivalent must be acceptable to the community:

English:   half-blood *n* [the relationship between individuals having only one parent in common]

Afrikaans:   halwe bloed [met een gemeenskaplike ouer]

Sepedi:   morwarre[16]

---

16   An equivalent with exactly the same meaning as the English does not exist in Sepedi owing to cultural differences. All the children in one family (Afrikaans: gesin) are brothers and sisters, irrespective of the fact that some of the members of this family may have only one parent in common. The term *hlaba* has a negative connotation, as it could be used for an illegitimate child. *Hlaba* is used in fighting language, for example when one contends for a higher position, for instance for chieftainship. The context will determine which term (*morwarre* or *hlaba*) to use.

Cultural differences may entail a difference in concept definition, for example the term **prostitute** (Skramstad 1990:106):
- **Prostitute:** In the English or another European language context this term:
   (1) coincides with the exchange of sexual services for money or goods between two or more people (Day 1988: 421–428), and
   (2) may refer to a man or a woman

- **Prostitute:** In the Gambian context this term [**Wolof***: chagga; **Mandinka***: cakoo] (*African languages)
   (1) applies only to a woman – but with a different definition from that of a prostitute in Western countries, and
   (2) a Gambian woman is labelled a prostitute if her conduct includes one or more of the following activities:
      (i)   the exchange of sexual services for money or goods
      (ii)  living unmarried
      (iii) wearing trousers
      (iv)  smoking in public
      (v)   drinking beer
      (vi)  walking with a man who is not the woman's kin, husband or husband's friend, or
      (vii) walking around too much

### 5.1.3 Interrelationship of terms

The various concepts belonging to a specific subject or domain have to be collected in a systematic way because terms stand in a specific relation to other terms. It is only by dealing with the various related terms and concepts as a whole that the terminologists can ensure the correct naming of concepts. This can be illustrated with the term **common law**:

| English | Afrikaans | Sepedi |
|---|---|---|
| common law[17] | gemene reg | molao wo o sego wa ngwalwa |
| common law[18] (general law) | gemene reg | molao wa bohle nageng |
| Common Law[19] | Common Law | Molao wa setlwaedi / Molaotwaedi |
| common-law marriage | gemeenregtelike huwelik | lenyalo la molaotlwaedi |
| common-law wife[20] | gemeenregtelike vrou | mosadi |

One should realise that it is often the relation between plain language words (eg words borrowed from the general language) and terms (belonging to a given sub-language) that pose the biggest problems:

| | |
|---|---|
| **English** | concubine |
| **Afrikaans** | bywyf, houvrou, konkubine |
| **Sepedi** | motlabo, nyatsi |
| **Swati** | makhwapheni |
| **Venda** | mufarekano, mudavhu, nyadzi |
| **Tsonga** | xigangu |

---

17  In South Africa the common law is based on Roman Dutch law.
18  There was a suggestion that *molao wa mmuso* be used as an equivalent for *common law* (general law), but it was felt that *molao wa mmuso* refers to *public law*, which governs the relationship between the state and its subjects or between government institutions *inter se*, and not to the relationship between people. Common law in this sense refers to the law that applies to all inhibitants of the country.
19  The Common Law system originated from the British legal tradition in contradistinction to Civil Law (Roman Law).
20  In African customary law the common-law wife is regarded as a marriage partner with full marital status because lobola has been paid for her. She is regarded in a totally different light from a concubine whose relationship may be of a temporary nature.

### 5.1.4 Source and target languages

Terminologists usually work from a specific **source language (SL)**. In South Africa the source language is usually English and term equivalents have to be supplied in the other official South African languages.

It is necessary to remember that in South Africa, Afrikaans and the other indigenous languages are all minority languages compared with a dominant language such as English that is used worldwide. Minority languages like Afrikaans and the African languages find it very difficult to create a scientific and technical terminology next to the existing terminology of the dominant English language. There are certain **cultural**, **political** and **economic** factors inhibiting or impeding the coining and penetration of terms in the minority languages. One should try to understand that it is not only difficult to communicate without proper knowledge of the various indigenous languages and lack of training in terminological principles, but there are also several other difficulties and obstacles that have to be dealt with by terminologists if they want to provide acceptable multilingual terminology.

No language exists in isolation. Various cultures and language communities have an influence on one another. Originally Sepedi, for instance, had no use for the letters $v$, $x$ and $q$. At present these consonants are used for click sounds in borrowed words (loan words) with click sounds: for example **nxanxae**: verskoning vra, pardon.

Furthermore, one should also keep in mind that although terms do in fact exist in the various languages these terms are, however, not documented and therefore not standardised. If a new concept was not previously named in a language, a term has to be created.

### 5.1.5 Term creation

Anyone designating concepts by means of terms must be sure of the underlying meaning of the concept before coining a term. Term creation can be fun if one is able to create catchy terms, for example the English "**fat cat**" became "**roomvraat**" in Afrikaans, or the Afrikaans "**gabbaïsme**" for the English term "**cronyism**" (crony = gabba). But beware, it is sometimes more difficult to get term equivalents for plain language words than for proper scientific or highly technical terms. Is the English "**town**" (Afrikaans: "**dorp**") for instance a synonym for the English "**city**" (Afrikaans: "**stad**")?

No? Then why do we have Cape **Town** / Kaap**stad**; Grahams**town** / Graham**stad**, London **Town**?

Although Afrikaans has a long terminology tradition, it is sometimes difficult to get a translation equivalent for plain English terms:

English: hit *n* <slang> [a murder carried out as the result of an underworld vendetta or rivalry]

Afrikaans: huurmoord (?)

Sepedi: polaotlhoyo[21] [a killing committed out of hatred]

polaorongwa [a killing when someone has been sent, or contractually employed to kill another; a killing when a killer is hired to assassinate someone (Afrikaans: sluipmoord, huurmoord)]

polaopakišano

~~polaonkwa~~

Changed to: polaokwanelwa

One should also take the orthographical rules of a language into consideration when coining terms. When working in a language with a disjunctive orthography, one cannot provide **a single equivalent word** for a given term in the same way as in a language with a conjunctive orthography. The Afrikaans orthography allows for a conjunctive manner of writing and therefore Afrikaans terms tend to be one word. English and some of the orthographies of the African languages prescribe a disjunctive manner of writing and therefore the terms tend to consist of more than one word. Although terms may consist of more than one word in the African languages, these can still be regarded as terms since the orthographies prescribe disjunctive writing. Language users will have to choose between the literal translation equivalent on the one hand, that is a transliteration [such as *ikopi* (English: copy)], that might have an equal number of words in all the African languages, or a conceptual equivalent which will not have an equal number of words in all the African languages. A conceptual equivalent may be unrecognisable at the first glance, but may be more user-friendly to the target group. Even Afrikaans, being conjunc-

---

21 "Hit" could have more than one meaning – the context would dictate which term to use.

tive, had to compromise whenever words became either too long, or had to be (inter)nationally recognisable, as in Physics, Chemistry, and so on:

English: hit list (**disjunctive**)

Afrikaans: huurmoordlys (**conjunctive**)

Sepedi: lenaneo la polaorongwa [this term could also refer to the plans or tactics that are going to be used]

lenaneoina la polaorongwa [a list of people to be murdered] (**disjunctive**)

Terms are not created in a haphazard way. There are specific ways of supplying term equivalents in the various languages, such as borrowing, transliteration, neologisms, etc. Terminologists, subject specialists and linguists who have to supply term equivalents for source language terms have a variety of ways to apply, namely:

- **loan words** (from English, Dutch, Flemish, German, French (mainly European languages) *(affidavit / affidavit / afidavite; Hansard / Hansard / Hansard, Hansate; abortus / abortus / abortuse)*

  The principle is to use at the Greek or Latin origin of the term. The term equivalent (eg Sepedi equivalent), must be congruent with the source language. The *ff* combination is not normally used in African languages. According to the Sepedi rule a consonant must be followed by a vowel and one should adhere to the rules of the specific language, therefore *afidavite*.

  The term "Hansard" (Eng/Afr) [the official published report of proceedings in the British Parliament, named after Luke Hansard (1752 – 1828) and his descendants who compiled and printed the journals of the House of Commons until 1889] was borrowed in Sepedi: *Hansard, Hansate* (synonym (according to Sepedi orthography).

  Certain terms (as with *abortus: abortus: abortuse*) are sensitive and form part of mainly women's language in African culture. They are not part of the natural language of all the people. The idiomatic expression *lefolotsana* that is used for animals, when applied to humans, is obscene. *Pholotswa* can be used to make it more acceptable.

* **transliteration** (using the Greek or Latin stem to coin an equivalent) (**addendum L** neutral of *addendus*: addendum

/ toevoeging / adentamo (tlalletso); bail ME *bail, baille*, from **MF** *bail*, from *bailler* to give, deliver, from L *bajulare* to bear a burden, keep in custody, from *bajulus porter, load carrier*: bail / borg / peile)

The source language (English) was used to coin the term equivalent. A "p" was used in Sepedi instead of a "b" to get the right pronunciation.

- **total embedding or adoption of a term in its original form without transliteration**
  The original term usually stems from Latin. The term is embedded in the target language without changing or adapting any part of the original (SL) term. The terms are usually explained in the target language to enable users to use it appropriately.
- **extension of meaning** (using existing words but broadening the meaning to encompass the new concept) *(abet / aanmoedig / go thusana le go thusa bosenying; abductor / ontvoerder / motshabisamongwe)*.

  The Sepedi equivalent of "abductor" literally means a person who steals another person –*thopa* (captives in a war). This meaning is foreign to the Sotho group of languages. The concept is known in the Nguni tradition as *ukuthwala*. It has a positive meaning and is used when a man captures the girl he loves and intends to marry. The term *ukuthumba* has a negative meaning. Terminologists have to know the exact meaning to avoid ambiguity. In most cases the subject or the context determines the meaning and therefore determines the choice of a term.
- **neologisms** *(claim/kleim/kleime; adopt (child)/aanneem (kind)/ adopta (ngwana)*.

  *claim: kleim: kleime:* A new word had to be coined. In Sotho culture people do not claim something; they have a right to it.

  *adopt: aanneem: adopta:* This word is common in Western culture. In African culture a child can never be possessed by nursing and feeding it; a new word had to be coined.

### 5.1.6 Connotation

The terminologist should be sensitive not to incorporate offensive and/or sensitive items in a dictionary. Terminology is by nature

abstract and exact and it is therefore to a great extent secure against emotive connotations that can be attached to words. The legal domain overlaps to a certain extent with social and political subject fields and one has to be aware of the incorporation of potentially offensive and sensitive terms such as:
- *gewoonteverbintenis* or *gebruiklike verbinding*
  (English = customary union)
  degrading term for:
  *gewoonteregtelike huwelik* or *inheemsregtelike huwelik*
  (English: customary marriage or indigenous marriage)
  (Cf Act 38 of 1927 and Act 76 of 1963)
- *deelgenoot van 'n gebruiklike verbinding*
  (English = partner of a customary union)
  instead of
  *eggenoot van 'n inheemsregtelike huwelik*
  (English = spouse of a customary marriage)
- *toordokter* (witchdoctor)
  degrading term for:
  *tradisionele geneser* (traditional doctor)
  wrong term for *towenaar* (sorcerer)

### 5.1.7 Legal systems

The terminologist working with legal terminology in a multilingual society such as South Africa's encounters interesting problems. Although Roman Dutch Law forms the basis of the South African legal system, this system is also greatly influenced by *inter alia* British Common Law and Indigenous Law in an African context.

According to British Common Law two terms are used:

• libel = written    • slander = by word of mouth

According to South African law (traditional Roman Dutch Law), the term "defamation" is used for the **criminal offence**. No distinction is made between the written or that by word of mouth.

The various legal systems pose a serious problem when determining the exact meaning of a concept. It is therefore necessary to excerpt legal terms from existing documentation and first of all to define these concepts accurately in the South African context before it is possible to denote them with equivalents in any of the African languages. Different legal systems pose problems not only in South Africa, but also internationally. (TEPIS is an organisation working on the standardisation of Polish law terminology in English. Polish law is codified and both its concepts and the Polish terms are standardised. It is therefore possible to create a standard English terminology for Polish standardised legal concepts and terms.[22] In so far as legal systems are incompatible in principle this kind of secondary (foreign language) standardisation of a specific system-bound terminology may be valid only for users of such a primary system. In the TEPIS case, it may be useful for English-speaking foreigners interested in the Polish law system (eg for commercial or investment purposes) and for Poles dealing with such foreigners. Such secondary terminology must be based strictly on denotative equivalence and may only be used within the limited scope of dissemination.)

### 5.1.8 Penetration of terms

Only a term with an exact meaning will promote exact communication. According to Cluver[23] the standard view of the objectives of terminographical work on developed standard languages is on collecting terms and standardising them by a definition rather than on the creation of new terms.

When supplying or coining term equivalents the terminologists consult linguists. It is of great importance that linguists should comment on the terms to give authority to the term equivalents. By obtaining the consent of subject specialists as well as linguists the terms will be used by both experts and laypeople in the user's environment. Only terms that are both technically and linguistically sound will penetrate into a language and will be disseminated in the subject field through the language.

The terminologist should be aware of the sociolinguistic factors that play a role in the penetration of terms in a person's vocabulary. As soon as a person becomes familiar with a specific term, this term becomes part of his everyday vocabulary and in the process this term becomes a **word** and no longer a term belonging to the terminology of a specific subject field. When a term penetrates the general vocabulary it tends to lose the original and exact standardised meaning attached to the concept it denotes. The term becomes a word and its meaning may become narrower or may broaden in the general usage of colloquial language.

---

22 Kierzkowska 1999.
23 (1989) 247.

According to Fourie[24] several scholars have noted that not all terminology is accepted by speech communities. Reasons given for rejection are that:
- terminology is inexpressive and often nonsensical;[25]
- the relationship between terminological institution and language user is not based on feedback;
- terms are artificial or do not comply with folk taxonomy;[26]
- terms are cumbersome and unwieldy, and often seem not to be giving the correct meaning;[27] and
- there might be political, sociological, cultural, religious or psychological reasons for people not accepting new terms.[28]

Although Fourie[29] gives several reasons for the phenomenon of term rejection, two main reasons can be distinguished for this terminographic error. The first involves avoidable inaccuracies in the terminographic process, while the other relates to cognitive difficulties in the encoding and decoding process.

According to Fourie[30] the available terminology in African languages is sometimes rejected owing to the fact that terms are sometimes not sociolinguistically acceptable. This implies the culturally determined processing of terms by a particular speech community. Term rejection is sometimes due to the terminographical process where a term is incompatible with the subject for which it was coined.

The most prominent problem with regard to the terminographical process is that all possible concepts in a given subject field are not taken into account before coinage takes place.

A further problem is that it is often non-existing (European) concepts that are imported into African languages (eg high treason/hoogverraad for which no Sepedi concept could be found). This leads to a situation where coined terms are often rejected because transliterations of foreign terms are well established and accepted before terms are coined for the new concept:

---

24 (1994) 11.
25 Zimmerman (1987) 47.
26 Ohly (1987) 5.
27 Jafta (1987) 137.
28 Abdulaziz (1989) 45.
29 (1994) 14.
30 (1993) 11.

English   hitchhiker *n*
Afrikaans  ryloper
Sepedi:   mokgopelanametšo,[31] mosepelakamonwana (synonym); mohaeki (synonym, loan word)

English   homosexual n (general) [a person sexually attracted to somebody of the same sex]
Afrikaans  homoseksueel
Sepedi    morobalalewabongbjagwe
          lehomo[32] (synonym, loan word)
          lehomosektšhuale (synonym, loan word)

English   gay [a man who is sexually attracted to other men]
Afrikaans  homoseksueel
Sepedi    morobalalewabongbjagwebonna
          lekei (synonym, loan word)

English   lesbian [a woman who is sexually attracted to other women]
Afrikaans  lesbiër
Sepedi    morobalalewabongbjagwebosadi
          lelesbiene (synonym, loan word)

Another problem is that several terms denoting the same concept may be in popular use at the same time (English: bar code; Afrikaans: staafkode / strepieskode). This obviously weakens the technical language – which is meant to be a precise and exact register. It also to some extent forces either random use or the rejection of some of these terms.[33]

The use of traditional terms that through meaning shift acquire a new meaning (constituted by shifts in both sense and reference) may be the solution for term coinage. On the surface it appears as

---

31  The term mokgopela-go-nametšwa (a person who asks for a lift) was coined but it was decided that it was a literal translation and not a term.
32  The *le* class is used for matters unacceptable to the culture; *mo* is used for things out of the ordinary.
33  Fourie (1994) 12.

if the harmonisation principle of relying on language internal resources, that is using traditional terms as bases for terms, is a good idea. Among the reasons given are that no lexical pollution takes place and that the human brain, being a pattern finder, would relate better to language-internal resources owing to culture-specific thought patterns (in terms of understanding and memory).[34] According to Mochaba[35] these terms in practice sometimes also present a pitfall. He observes several Sesotho terms based on traditional terms, and cannot see any connection or association between the new and old referents and the concepts for which they stand. He further notes that these terms are remote from the experiences of ordinary language users, and were not listed in dictionaries, and that there is no justification for the relationships between the traditional and modern referents. Fourie[36] notes that the cognitive reasoning which is meant to establish the concept-term assignment is criticised in terms of the cultural acceptability of the link between the source concept (traditional) and the new concept.

The terminographic process dealing with concept definitions also poses some problems when there is a difference between the cultures of the source language (SL) and that of the target language (TL).[37] A second type of difference in concept definition occurs between that which the term denotes and that which the term is meant to denote.

The generally preferred explanatory coinage method in practice implies descriptive terms, that at a more refined level contract to shorter forms. The problem with descriptive terms is that they comprise simplified wordings of given conceptual definitions which leaves several premises for misinterpretation.

One type of terminological error involves the predicted meaning shift that occurs between a new term and a new concept. Here the term assigned to a particular source concept undergoes meaning shift in the process of successful coinages, in order for that term (or a term based on that native root) to reflect a new concept in a particular language, in such a way that the meaning shift is transparent and acceptable for a particular speech community.

The error involves the coinage of a term that does not sustain a successful and acceptable meaning shift between source concept and (new) target concept, and results in the consequent rejection of the officially coined term by a particular speech community.

---

34  Fourie (1994) 12.
35  (1987) 143.
36  (1994) 12.
37  Fourie (1994) 13.

## 5.2 Multilingualism: harmonisation/unification?

Multilingualism in any given country is still seen by many people as a problem. To a certain extent this is true: it is just not possible to translate all official documents into eleven languages. At this stage it is also impossible since the terminology in most subject fields is non-existent for all or most of the indigenous languages except Afrikaans.[38]

Factors that limit terminology development are organisational structures and bureaucracy. These limit the efficiency of terminography and term dissemination instead of optimising these activities. Perhaps this situation can be rectified in future since the Terminology Division of the National Language Service of the Department of Arts, Culture, Science and Technology has as one of its objectives the creation and dissemination of terminology in all the official languages.

A factor that may in future have a radical influence on terminology is harmonisation that can be explained as the creation of one standard language formed by related languages of the Sotho and Nguni families respectively. Academics differ considerably regarding the viability of harmonisation.

Cluver[39] sees "the unification of various closely related varieties into a standard language" as one of the solutions for the "problem" of multilingualism. Some academics,[40] however, regard unification or harmonisation as a "disturbing development … which … will undoubtedly hamper the development of such a renewed linguistic nationalism in South Africa". According to Louwrens,[41] the strongest version of the harmonisation movement (the Nhlapo/ Alexander scenario) has as its aim "the orthographic, lexical and grammatical harmonisation of, for example, Northern Sotho (Sepedi), Southern Sotho (Sesotho) and Western Sotho (Setswana) into one so-called Standard Sotho "language" of unpredictable composition.

A weaker and probably more realistic version aims at the harmonisation of, for example, the three main Sotho languages and the four main Nguni languages at the orthographic and terminological levels only.[42]

---

38  Cf Alberts (1998) 231.
39  (1994) 168.
40  Cf Louwrens (1996) 3.
41  Ibid 3.
42  Cf Alberts (1998) 231-232.

Nahir[43] defines terminology unification or harmonisation as "establishing unified terminologies, mostly technical, by clarifying and defining them, in order to reduce communicative ambiguity ...". According to Cluver[44] this objective coincides with the standard view of the objectives of terminological work on developed standard languages. The focus here is on collecting terms and standardising them by a definition rather than on the creation of new terms.

## 5.3  Internationalisation of terms

The International Organisation for Unification of Terminological Neologisms (IOUTN) compiled a World Bank of International Terms (WBIT). The IOUTN has been affiliated to the United Nations as a non-governmental organisation since 1987. The IOUTN affiliates philologists, linguists and specialists in various fields of science and technology who are interested in problems of transnationalisation and dissemination of specialised terminology. The main task of the IOUTN is to encourage the borrowing of specialised terminology from the language of its creators and to stimulate consciousness in all countries that this action is in every nation's interest.

The IOUTN publishes glossaries and vocabularies to facilitate the work of translators, interpreters, writers and workers in various domains. It aims to transfer all the latest specialised terminology to less developed and developing countries. The WBIT within the IOUTN engages in accumulating and storing international terminology and specialised neologisms using the materials supplied by more than 200 members from 40 countries all over the world. Incidentally, it is the first term bank in the world to hold a catalogue of multilingual international terms.[45]

The spin-off of the WBIT is a series of dictionaries of international terms with international specialised terminology that can be used by those interested in particular fields. These dictionaries have to play a double role: practical and theoretical. Their practicality lies in the fact that the scientist or translator/interpreter can find transnational equivalents in the respective domain and language. Regarding the theoretical aspects, these dictionaries will

---

43  (1984) 308.
44  (1989) 247.
45  Stoberski (1998) 6.

demonstrate to the interested persons how international scientific and technical terminology has already developed.

There are millions of international scientific and technical terms available in various languages. These are convenient to use as they mostly have common definitions and are similar or identical in external form. They facilitate the international exchange of human knowledge in all fields. The number of specialised terms in an average natural language is several times greater than the number of words in everyday use. If laypeople, or even linguists and professionals in various fields would realise that, they would not oppose the practice of borrowing specialised neologisms from the languages they were first used in Stoberski.[46]

Professor Stoberski plans a World Encyclopaedia of International Terms with definitions not only in English, but in French, German, Polish, Russian, Spanish and later also in Arabic and Chinese, and so on. It is envisaged that the official South African languages will also be included in future publications.

It seems to be difficult to internationalise legal terminology within the traditional definition of "internationalisation" since international legal systems do not appear to be compatible. Any legal terminological system must begin the process of its internationalisation with the internationalisation of its concepts. The easiest way to achieve this is to build a primary and a secondary system of legal terminology concurrently. This occurs in countries such as Canada and Finland, where legal regulations are passed simultaneously in English and French or in Finnish and Swedish. It is also the case with the European Union which does not need to be internationalised because it is international by definition.[47]

Full internationalisation of national legal terminologies will, according to Kierzkowska (1999), never be possible. It will, though, certainly be possible in the future gradually to internationalise systems of legal concepts to be followed by the gradual internationalisation of national terminologies. Before they become universal, terminologists should apply existing internationalisms, exchange their national terminologies on a worldwide scale and support every effort made towards internationalisation and standardisation of legal concepts.

These international projects indicate that there is a worldwide trend in terminology to internationalise terms in a variety of subjects – even in the domain of the legal sub-language. Internatio-

---

46 (1998) 3.
47 Kierzkowska (1999).

nalised terms are still spelt according to the orthography of the specific languages but by sharing the same stem one can recognise the terms, with a knowledge of the subject field, can easily derive the meanings attached to the terms. This leads to better communication worldwide.

### 5.4 The effect of harmonisation/unification and internationalisation on terminology development

Possibilities for harmonisation/unification and internationalisation in the field of terminology is conceivable although much research still has to be done in this regard.

The terminology/terminography process in South Africa favours English. English is regarded as the source language since it is through the medium of English that most terms reach South Africa. Once the English terms are excerpted and supplied with a definition or example sentence they can be given with equivalents in the ten indigenous languages. Traditionally the English terms were given Afrikaans equivalents only but since South Africa now has eleven official languages the English terms must be supplied with term equivalents in the other ten official languages.

The terminologist usually concentrates on the standard variety of a language. Various non-standard languages are developing owing to extensive contact between speakers of different African languages as well as to a changing environment. Within the current education system, the increasing use of non-standard language in the classroom often has dire consequences for learners and for the traditional language.[48]

In South Africa a spontaneous process of harmonisation is taking place in townships where various language groups merge. Schuring's[49] study on Pretoria Sotho is conclusive proof of this. His findings were that the Pretoria Sotho is a mixture of Kgatla, Pedi and Tswana dialects, as well as adoptives from English and Afrikaans. In this case the principles of harmonisation (eg search for an existing word in the various dialects or related languages) are applied. It should, however, always be established whether this is what the users want.

In the harmonising of related languages, the terminologist should adopt a descriptive approach rather than a prescriptive one. In this instance the terminologist documents the terminology used

---

48 Calteaux (1996).
49 (1984).

by the language users and by so doing he or she will then standardise the harmonised form. When one listens to the vocabulary of people at grassroots level, the jargon that they use actually becomes prototypical terminology. The terminologist should document these terms rather than try to coin new terms that might never be used by the target group, be they people at grassroots level, scientists or technologists.

Although in the past the seven language boards concerned with terminology functioned as separate institutions, a degree of harmonisation resulted from similar or even identical terms coined by them, for example terms for school, brick, book, pen, television, radio, copy, and so on. It should, however, be noted that some of these terms were later substituted with other coinages.

| | | |
|---|---|---|
| **English** | school | brick |
| **Afrikaans** | skool | baksteen |
| **Ndebele** | isikolo | isitina |
| **Swati** | sikolo | sitini |
| **Xhosa** | isikolo | isitena |
| **Zulu** | isikolo | isitini |
| **Sepedi** | sekolo | setena |
| **Sesotho** | sekolo | setene |
| **Tswana** | sekolo | setena |
| **Venda** | tshikolo | tshidina |
| **Tsonga** | xikolo | xitina |

When coining terms (neologisms) for new concepts in any of the South African official languages it is of the utmost importance to consult the other languages to see whether the concept has already been named. By consulting the other languages it is much easier for the terminologist to coin a new term in the relevant language according to the existing terms in the other language(s). This is one of the main objectives of harmonisation – to make use of the existing words in the standard variety of a language as well as in its dialects rather than to coin a completely new term. The terminologist will maintain the language and will at the same time develop it by extending the meaning of an existing word in the standard form or dialect to match the meaning of a new concept.

An area where the principles of harmonisation or internationalisation can be applied is in the development of technical Nguni and Sotho languages. Since the Nguni and Sotho cultural languages have a sizeable core of common vocabularies, it would be ideal if they also had a common pool of technical terminologies[50]. In this case terms for modern concepts can generally be shared by the Nguni and Sotho groups. It will then not be necessary to coin separate terms for Ndebele, Swati, Xhosa and Zulu (Nguni group) or for Sepedi, Sesotho, Setswana (Sotho group). A team of terminologists for all the Nguni languages and one for the Sotho languages (consisting of representatives for the separate languages within the specific language group) can work together when denoting concepts.

Terminology can, to a certain extent, be regarded as an artificial language. To introduce harmonisation/unification or internationalisation in the terminology process will not be a foreign principle. Since terminology is mainly interested in written language the principles of harmonisation and internationalisation can be applied here. It is also merely concerned with the naming of new concepts. A basic "recognisable" term can be coined and adjusted to the orthography rules of the different languages. The term will be nationally (and internationally) recognisable since it will consist of the basic stem with language-specific adjustments.

As far as terminology and terminography are concerned it can be concluded that harmonisation and internationalisation are possible. Terminology and terminography provide a favourable situation for coining terms in African languages since new terms have to be coined to accommodate new concepts. Rather than naming every new concept with a totally different term, it is sensible to coin terms according to the group pattern and not necessarily according to the individual languages. Likewise it is possible when coining new terms in Sotho to do it in accordance with the Sotho pattern and not that of Sesotho, Sepedi and Setswana as such. Terms can also be borrowed from the language of origin to make them internationally recognisable.

---

50  Msimang (1996) 20

## 6   Conclusion

Legal language is difficult to comprehend. Besides, it takes years of training and experience for lawyers to acquire and use legal language properly. There are reasons why it will be difficult to change legal language. These stem from a general misunderstanding of what makes language complex. Most institutions like legislatures, government agencies, insurance companies, and so on, which have attempted to simplify legal language have tried to experiment with readability formulas in the misapprehension that the number of syllables per word and the number of words per sentence are accurate indicators of the comprehensibility of a document. Unfortunately readability is not equivalent to comprehensibility. The situation is much more complex.

To my mind the solution to the problem does not lie in the legal terminology as such, but in the lack of proper definitions for legal concepts. A term in any language is just a few letters put together to denote a given concept. People will understand the legal concepts if they are properly defined – especially if the concepts are defined in a low register to enhance intelligibility. If people understand the underlying concept, they will be able to denote it in any language!

The idea of changing legal language into plain language to enable ordinary people to understand complex legal concepts seems to be gaining ground. If legal terminology is really to become accessible to laypeople, both the legal expert and the layperson should acknowledge certain points:[51]

- Legal language **is** appropriate for lawyers and other legal experts to use in communicating with other members of the legal community.
- It is possible to acquire information through **formal terminology** that is properly **defined.**
- Legal experts should simplify legalese when communicating with members of the general public to empower them.
- Laypeople have a responsibility to familiarise themselves with the law and with the more common legal terms.
- Laypeople should not be afraid to demand clarification when necessary.
- Legal experts should co-operate in the process of giving laypeople more access to legal concepts, for without the co-operation of the legal community it would be impossible for laypeople to gain access to legal language.

---

51   Cf Charrow, Crandall & Charrow (1982).

## 7    Bibliography

Abdulaziz, M H "Development of scientific and technical terminology with special reference to African languages" (1989) *Kiswahili* 56

Alberts, M (1990) *'n Bepaling van Afrikaanse vakleksikografiese behoeftes* Dlitt et Phil thesis, University of South Africa, Pretoria

Alberts, M (1996) *The harmonisation of Nguni and Sotho: Terminological Perspectives* (Paper read by invitation at the Pre-Seminar Colloquium on the Harmonisation and standardisation of African Languages for Education and Development, 11–13 July 1996, University of Cape Town, Cape Town)

Alberts, M (1997a) *Legalese: South Africa's 12th official language?* (Paper read by invitation at the Seminar on Language in Court at the former Venda Parliament (Government Buildings), Thohoyandou, 16–17 May 1997 The seminar was organised by the Northern Province Department of Education, Arts, Culture and Sports)

Alberts, M (1997b) Legal Terminology in African Languages *Lexikos 7* Afrilex series 7 (1997) 179–191

Alberts, M "The Harmonisation of Nguni and Sotho: Terminological Perspectives" in Prah, K K (1998) *Between Distinction & Extinction. The Harmonisation & Standardisation of African Languages.* Johannesburg: Witwatersrand University Press 229–242

Alexander, N (1989) *Language policy and national unity in South Africa/Azania* Cape Town: Buchu Books

Bix, B (1993) *Law, Language and Legal Determinacy* New York: Oxford University Press

Calteaux, K. (1996). *Standard and non-standard African language varieties in the urban areas of South Africa* Stanon Main Report Pretoria: HSRC

Charrow, R & Charrow, V (1975) *An Investigation of Jury Instruction Comprehension* Paper presented at the 4th Annual NWAVE Colloquium, Georgetown University, Washington DC, October, 1975

Charrow, V & Charrow, R (1976) *Investigating Comprehension in Real-World Tasks* Paper presented at the Linguistic Society of America Annual Meeting, Philadelphia, December, 1976

Charrow, V R, Crandall, J A & Charrow, R P "Characteristics and Functions of Legal Language" in Kittredge, R & Lehberger, J (1982) *Sublanguage. Studies of Language in Restricted Semantic Domains* Berlin Walter de Gruyter 175–190

Cluver, A D de V "A sociolinguistic approach to the study of technical languages" *Logos* (1987) 7(2) 13–30

Cluver, A D de V (1989) *A Manual of Terminography* Pretoria: HSRC

Cluver, A D de V (1994) Preconditions for language unification *South African Journal of Linguistics, Supplement* 20 168–194

Cluver, A D de V (1996) *Language development* Proceedings of a Langtag Workshop on Issues in Language Development: Focussing on The Future of the Apartheid language Boards and the Harmonisation and Development of African Languages 28 March 1996, Unisa, Pretoria

Felber, H (1982) *Basic principles and methods for the preparation of terminology standards* Vienna: Infoterm

Felber, H "Worldwide Efforts to Establish Principles and Methods in Terminology and Terminography" *TermNet News* (1996) 54/55:24-25

Fourie, D J "The rejection of terminology: Observations from the African languages" *South African Journal for African Languages* (1994) 12(1) 11–15

Galinski, C & Schmitz, K-D (eds) (1996) *TKE '96: Terminology and Knowledge Engineering* Frankfurt/M: Indeks Verlag

Jafta, N "The development of terminology in Xhosa: a case study" *Logos* (1987) 7(2)

Jansen, M (1992) *Double, Double Toil and Trouble – The problems encountered when compiling alegal dictionary in African Languages* Paper read at the ILLA Conference at the HSRC, Pretoria

Kierzkowska, D "Standardisation of Polish legal terminology" *Terminology* (1995) 2(1) 129–140

Kierzkowska, D (1999) Polskie Towarzystwo Tlumaczy Ekonomicznych, Praniczychi Sadowych, Czlonek Miedzynarodowej Federacji Tlumaczy Fit Rada Naczelna (Fax received on 29th June 1999 from Polish Society of Economic, Legal and Court Translators (TEPIS))

Kittredge, R & Lehrberger, J (1982) *Sublanguage. Studies of Language in Restricted Semantic Domains* Berlin: Walter de Gruyter

Lantag (1995) *Towards a National Plan for South Africa. A Report of the Language Plan Task Group* Pretoria: Department of Arts, Culture, Science and Technology

Lestrade, G P "Some reflections on the future of the South African Bantu languages" *Linguistic Studies* (1935) 13(2)

Lombard, D P, Van Wyk, E B & Mokgokong, P C (1985) *Introduction to the grammar of Northern Sotho*. Pretoria: JL van Schaik

Louwrens, L J (1994) *Dictionary of Northern Sotho grammatical terms* Pretoria: Via Afrika

Louwrens, L J (1996) *On the development of scientific terminology in African languages: The terminographer's dilemma in a new dispensation* Paper read at the first International Conference of the African Association for Lexicography (Afrilex), 1–2 July 1996, Rand Afrikaans University, Johannesburg

Mellinkoff, D (1963) *The Language of the Law* Boston: Little, Brown and Company

Mochaba, M B " 'Shift in meaning' in Sesotho modern terminology" *Logos* (1987) 7(2)

Msimang, C T (1994) Language attitudes and the harmonisation of Nguni and Sotho *South African Journal of Linguistics, Supplement* 20:147–167

Msimang, C T (1996) *The Nature and History of Harmonisation* Proceedings of a Langtag Workshop on Issues in Language Development: Focussing on The Future of the Apartheid language Boards and the Harmonisation and Development of African Languages 28 March 1996, Unisa, Pretoria

Mtintsilana, P N & Morris, R "Terminography in African languages in South Africa" *South African Journal of African Languages* (1988) 8(4) 109-113

Nahir, M "Language planning goals: a classification *Language problems and language planning* (1984) 8(3) 294–327

Nhlapo, J M (1944) *Bantu Babel* Cape Town: The African Bookman

Nkondo, C P N "Problems of terminology in African languages with special reference to Xitsonga" *Logos* (1987) 7(2) 69–78

O'Barr, W M (1982) *Linguistic Evidence* New York: Academic Press, Inc

Ohly, R "Corpus planning, glottoeconomics and terminography" *Logos* (1987) 7(2)

Poulos, G & Louwrens, L J (1994) *A linguistic analysis of Northern Sotho* Pretoria: Via Afrika

Prah, K K (1998) *Between Distinction & Extinction The Harmonisation & Standardisation of African Languages* Johannesburg: Witwatersrand University Press

Redish, J C "Readability" in Mac Donald, D A (1979) *Drafting Documents in Plain Language* New York, NY: Practising Law Institute

Schauer, F (1993) *Law and Language* England: Dartmouth Publishing Company Ltd

Schuring, G K (1984) *Omgangs-Sotho van die Swart Woongebiede van Pretoria* D.Litt. et Phil Thesis Johannesburg: Rand Afrikaans University

Schweighofer, E & Scheithauer, D "Legal Terminology Research in an Internet/WWW Environment" in Galinski, C & Schmitz, K-D (eds) (1996) *TKE '96: Terminology and Knowledge Engineering* Frankfurt am Main: Indeks Verlag 59–73

Stoberski, Z (1998) *Multilingual Dictionary of International terms* Warszawa: World Bank of International Terms (WBIT) within International Organization for Unification of Terminological Neologisms (IOUTN)

Van Schalkwyk, D J "Professional terminology in African languages: Theory and practice" *Logos* (1987) 7(2) 9–11

Zimmerman, W "What kind of terminology service for Third World languages?" *Logos* (1987) 7(2)

Zungu, P J N (1995) *Language variation in Zulu: a case study of contemporary codes and registers in the greater Durban area* D.Litt. et Phil. University of Durban Westville, Durban

# E
# Research on plain legal language in South Africa

E.1 Plain language in South Africa: Report on an empirical research project — page 121

## E.1
# Plain language in South Africa: Report on an empirical research project[1]

**Frans Viljoen**
Faculty of Law, University of Pretoria

**Annelize Nienaber**
Faculty of Law, University of Pretoria

| | |
|---|---|
| 1 | Introduction ... *page 121* |
| 2 | Attitudes towards legal language ... *page 122* |
| 3 | Accessibility of legal language: Births and Deaths Registration Act 51 of 1992 ... *page 129* |
| 4 | Recommendations ... *page 133* |

## 1    Introduction

At the beginning of 1998, the Centre for Science Development, the Human Sciences Research Council (HSRC), now the National Research Foundation (NRF), awarded us a grant to do empirical research into the accessibility of legal language in South Africa. We were particularly interested in the language of the law as we both hold post graduate degrees in a language in addition to our qualifications in law. This project offered us the opportunity to combine our interest in language with our training in law.

In order to research developments and trends in the field of plain legal language, we undertook brief study tours to Australia and the United States of America.[2] On our return we set out to design the research project. We subdivided the project into two sections or two sets of questions for which we needed answers.

---

[1] The Centre for Science Development, HSRC, funded the project with a grant.
[2] For some empirical research done in the USA, see eg Benson, R W and Kessler, J B "Legalese v Plain English: An empirical study of persuasion and credibility in appellate brief writing" (1987) 20 *Loyola of Los Angeles Law Review* 301. For empirical research done in Australia, see eg McKillop, B "What lawyers think about plain legal language" (1994) *Law Society Journal* 68 – 69.

We isolated the following questions:
- What are the attitudes of persons in the legal profession (judges, magistrates, lawyers, legal academics, law students) towards plain legal language? What are the reasons for their attitudes?[3] What are the attitudes of the general public to texts written in plain legal language? What are the reasons for their attitudes? Do the attitudes of the general public differ from the attitudes of legal professionals? Why, or why not?
- Does the general public find texts written in plain language easier to understand than those written in legal language? Should texts written in plain legal language be found to be more easily comprehensible, which specific factors (such as language or structure) impede comprehension the most?

What follows is a discussion of our research. We have divided our discussion into two sections, each section dealing with a different area of focus where we try to arrive at an answer to each of the questions mentioned above.

## 2 Attitudes towards legal language

### 2.1 Two judgments[4]

#### 2.1.1 Method

To test the attitudes of legal practitioners to the use of plain language in a reported judgment of a court case, we rewrote the judgment in *S v Jackson* 1998 (2) SA 984 (SCA) in plain language.[5] Ques-

---

3 For previous research on similar lines, see Kimble, J "Writing for dollars, writing to please" (1996–1997) 6 *The Scribes Journal of Legal Writing*, especially 24–25.
4 Joe Kimble's ideas inspired this part of the research.
5 The redraft is not a blueprint. We have used some of the plain legal language tenets to redraft. As anyone comparing the two drafts will see, the simplification consists of the following: inserting headings and numbering of paragraphs; a reorganised structure; shortened paragraphs and sentences; ridding the judgment of what may be considered excess detail; the use of bullets to enhance clarity. We also inserted a "question of law". All this is by no means novel. The Constitutional Court judges number the paragraphs in their judgments. Sometimes they also use headings. For an earlier use of headings in law reports, see *Blyth v Van den Heever* 1980 1 SA 191 (A) and *Standard Chartered Bank of Canada v Nepperm Bank* 1994 4 SA 747 (A). See also Gibbs, H "Judgment writing" (1993) 67 *Australian Law Journal* 494.

tionnaires were drawn up. The questionnaires required respondents to indicate which judgment (original or plain language version) they preferred (Appendix A to this article). These questionnaires were sent to judges, magistrates and other members of the legal profession.

The training and years in the profession of the respondents varied significantly. To test their attitudes towards a legal text, respondents received two versions of the judgment and a questionnaire: the original *S v Jackson*, marked "V", as well as the simplified version, marked "W" (Appendix B to this article). The original judgment is not reprinted here, as it is readily available in the South African Law Reports. Respondents had to show their preference, and answer questions about the reason for their choice.

We mailed copies of the two versions with questionnaires attached to all advocates and judges practising in Pretoria and Johannesburg. We also randomly selected two first-year law classes (one English group, one Afrikaans) at the University of Pretoria. In total, we received back 382 completed questionnaires.

## 2.1.2 Results

### i Overall preference (Graph 1)

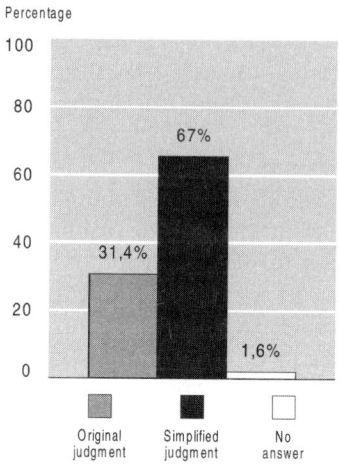

Original judgment:
 31,4% (total number = 120)
Simplified judgment:
 67% (total number = 256)
No answer:
 1,6% (total number = 6)

The respondents, as a group, preferred the simplified version. This result suggests that lawyers as a group prefer plain legal language.

### ii Preference according to years in legal profession (Graph 2)

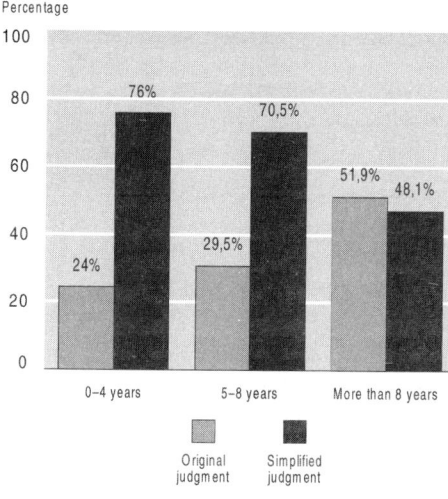

*0 – 4 years*
Original judgment:
 24% (total number = 59)
Simplified judgment:
 76% (total number = 187)

*5 – 8 years*
Original judgment:
 29,5% (total number = 5)
Simplified judgment:
 70,5% (total number = 12)

*More than 8 years*
Original judgment:
 51,9% (total number = 54)
Simplified judgment:
 48,1% (total number = 50)

It is clear that the longer a respondent has been part of the legal profession, the more supportive he or she is of traditional legal language.

## iii Preference according to profession (Graph 3)

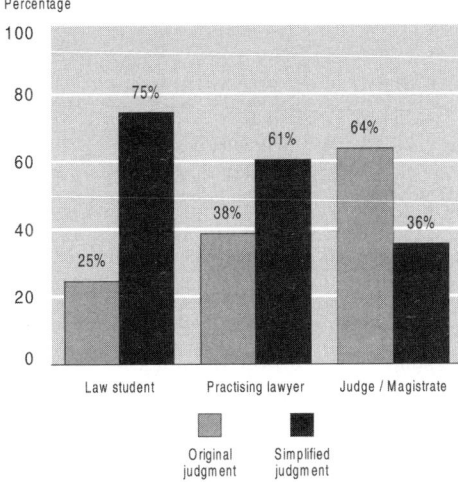

*Law student*
Original judgment:
 25% (total number = 58)
Simplified judgment:
 75% (total number = 174)

*Practising lawyer*
Original judgment:
 39% (total number = 39)
Simplified judgment:
 61% (total number = 61)

*Judge/Magistrate*
Original judgment:
 64% (total number = 21)
Simplified judgment:
 36% (total number = 12)

The results indicate resistance to plain legal language among judges and magistrates. It also correlates to some extent with the results in Graph 2.

## iv Preference according to race (Graph 4)

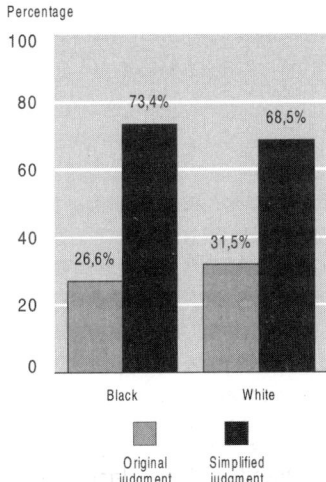

*Black*
Original judgment:
 26,6% (total number = 33)
Simplified judgment:
 73,4% (total number = 91)

*White*
Original judgment:
 31,5% (total number = 78)
Simplified judgment:
 68,5% (total number = 170)

It is clear that black as well as white respondents prefer the simplified version. However, there is a slightly greater preference for the simplified version among black respondents.

## 2.2 Two actions for divorce

### 2.2.1 Method

We used student assistants to administer questionnaires to a second group of respondents. These respondents had no legal training. We gave two versions of an "Action for Divorce" to each respondent. The first version ("A" attached hereto as Appendix C) is written in traditional legalese, and the second ("B" attached hereto as Appendix D) is written in simplified or "plain" legal language. Again, respondents had to show which of the two versions they preferred, and give a reason for their choice. We targeted randomly selected South Africans without a legal background. A total of 144 questionnaires were administered.

### 2.2.2 Results

**i    Overall preference** (Graph 5)

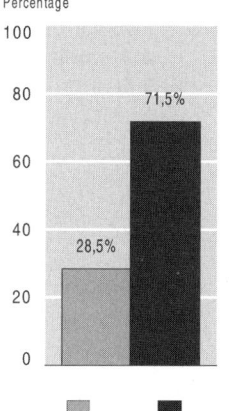

Traditional legalese:
   28,5% (total number = 41)
Simplified legal language:
   71,5% (total number = 103)

The results represented in Graph 5 show that non-lawyers prefer plain legal language to legalese. This result corresponds to the preference of lawyers for the simplified judgment (Graph 1). The margin in favour of plain legal language is slightly larger among non-lawyers than among lawyers (71,5% against 67%).

## ii  Preference according to gender (Graph 6)

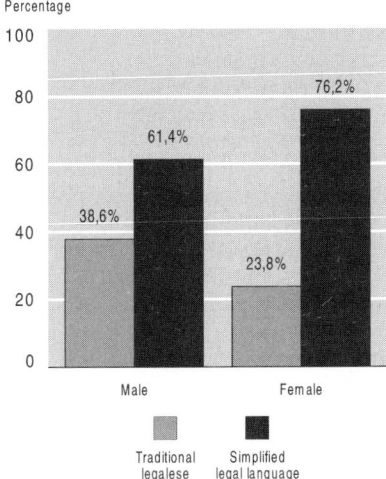

*Male*
Traditional legalese:
 38,6% (total number = 17)
Simplified legal language:
 61,4% (total number = 27)

*Female*
Traditional legalese:
 23,8% (total number = 24)
Simplified legal language:
 76,2% (total number = 77)

Female respondents showed a greater preference for the plain legal language version than male respondents.

## iii  Preference according to race (Graph 7)

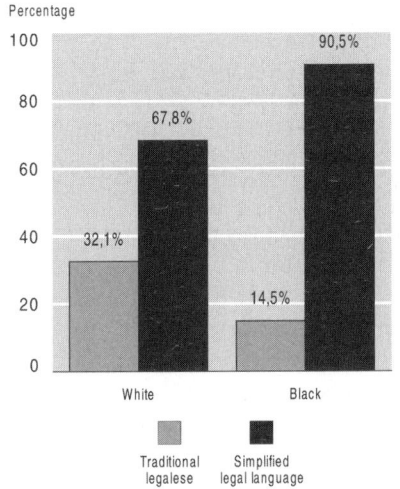

*White*
Traditional legalese:
 32,1% (total number = 37)
Simplified legal language:
 67,8% (total number = 78)

*Black*
Traditional legalese:
 14,5% (total number = 3)
Simplified legal language:
 90,5% (total number = 19)

Black respondents showed a greater preference for the plain legal language version, compared with white respondents.

### iv Preference according to educational level (Graph 8)

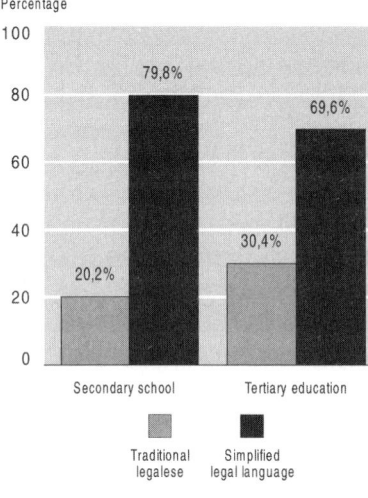

*Secondary School*
Traditional legalese:
  20,2% (total number = 20)
Simplified legal language:
  79,8% (total number = 79)

*Tertiary education*
Traditional legalese:
  30,4% (total number = 14)
Simplified legal language:
  69,6% (total number = 32)

Respondents with a secondary school education showed a greater preference for plain legal language than respondents with a tertiary qualification. However, respondents preferred the plain legal language version to the version in legalese, irrespective of their level of education.

## 2.3 Conclusion

To conclude, the following may be noted:
- Lawyers and non-lawyers prefer plain legal language.
- Black (predominantly non-mother tongue speakers of English) show a greater preference for the simpler versions than white respondents (whose mother tongue is more likely to be English).
- The younger respondents show a greater preference for simpler texts than the older respondents.
- The more educated the respondents are, the greater their preference for the original or legalese version.
- The female respondents show a greater preference for plain legal texts than the male respondents.
- The longer respondents have been in the legal profession, the greater their preference is for the original or legalese version.

Furthermore, on the basis of the above we conclude that simpler legal language will be accepted very positively by the vast majority of South Africans. Plain language will contribute towards greater access to the law, and may contribute towards solving the long-existing legitimacy crisis in the law.

## 3 Accessibility of legal language: Births and Deaths Registration Act 51 of 1992

### 3.1 Method

The aim of the questionnaire was to establish which factors were most significant in impeding the comprehension of legal texts. Two different factors were isolated:
- Language (grammar, sentence structure, vocabulary)
- Structure (overall structure of the section, for example, the use of different paragraphs and subsections to set out the content more clearly)

The questionnaire was distributed randomly to 60 adult South African respondents. Only respondents who had no formal legal training were selected.

Attempts were made to distribute the questionnaire to respondents of diverse and representative linguistic, cultural, educational and professional backgrounds.

Five versions of the text were used:
(i) the original version ("Original" in Graphs 10 and 11, "1" in Appendix E);
(ii) a version where only the language of the section, but not its structure, had been simplified ("Language" in Graphs 9 and 10, "2" in Appendix E);
(iii) a version where the overall structure of the section had been simplified, but not the language ("Structure" in Graphs 9 and 10, "3" in Appendix E);
(iv) another version where the simplified language and structure of (ii) and (iii) had been combined ("Structure & Language" in Graphs 9 and 10, "4" in Appendix E);
(v) a version that was reworked into plain language ("Plain Language" in Graphs 9, 10 and 11, "5" in Appendix E).

The questionnaire was structured as follows:
- Section A: Biographical data
- Section B: Section 11 (a) – (c) of the Act (reworked into the different versions), followed by a problem-type question based on the content of section 11.

We set a problem-type question to simulate the process the reader has to follow to gain information from legislation.[6] To arrive at the correct answer, respondents had to do the following:
- (a) Come to a general understanding of the content of section 11.
- (b) Work out what is required by the question.
- (c) Find the relevant information that is needed to answer the question.
- (d) Apply the information selected from the text to the problem.
- (e) Arrive at an answer.

Respondents were asked to write down not only their answers, but also the time that it took them to answer the question. We expected the level of difficulty experienced to be reflected in the time taken by each respondent to answer the question. There was no time limit set in which respondents had to answer the questions.

### 3.2   Results

When interpreting the respondents' answers, we were looking for one "correct" answer to our question, or a correct solution to our problem. However, we gave credit to responses that were too vague to be correct, but which nevertheless showed an understanding of the broad content of the section. We ignored any stylistic, grammar or spelling errors in the answers. The results of the answers to the questionnaire were as follows:

---

6   In this regard, see Prutting, E "Pragmatics as social competence" (1982) *Journal of Speech and Hearing Disorders* 25. Also see Bransford, R *et al* "Sentence memory: A constructive versus interpretive approach" (1972) *Cognitive Psychology* 193 – 209.

### 3.2.1 **Correct response frequencies** (Graph 9)

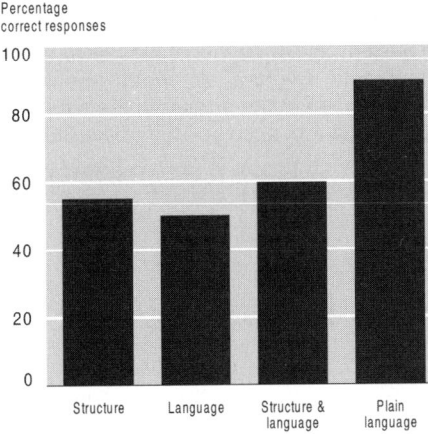

As was expected, the original version elicited the fewest number of correct responses and the plain language version the most. Structure was shown to be more significant in impeding comprehension than language. This is especially interesting as it debunks the popular fallacy that plain legal writing involves the substitution of "difficult" words with "easier" ones.

### 3.2.2 **Time taken to answer the question** (Graph 10)

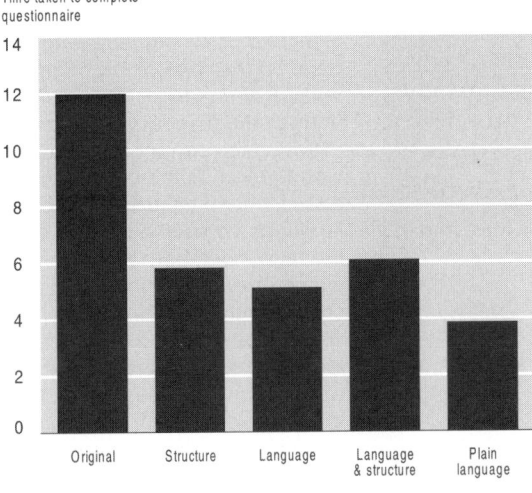

The average time taken by respondents to answer the question based on the original version of the Act was 12,02 minutes, while respondents who worked with the plain language version took 3,9 minutes to answer the question – almost a third of the time taken by the "original" group. This indicates that the accessibility of the text impacts directly on the time taken to arrive at an answer. Those groups who worked with the three versions where changes were made in the language and structure of the text took half the time taken by the group that worked with the original version:

- "Structure" group took an average of 5,8 minutes.
- "Language" group took an average of 5,2 minutes.
- "Language and structure" group took an average of 6,1 minutes.

You will note that the third group, the group that was given a version where both the language and structure had been simplified, took longer to answer the question than the groups where the language and structure were changed in isolation. It is furthermore interesting to note that even though the "original" group spent longer in answering the question, their answers were not correct. It actually appears that the longer a respondent spent on the question (finding and applying information to the problem), the smaller his or her chances were of providing the correct answer. This shows that there may be a critical point where the frustration or difficulty of deciphering the text makes it impossible for the reader to arrive at the correct answer.

### 3.2.3 Correlation between correct response frequency and linguistic background (Graph 11)

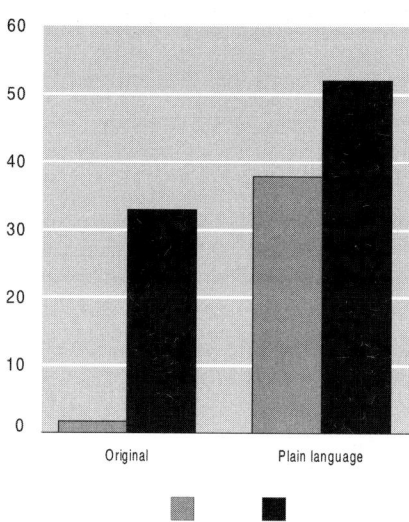

Correlation between correct response frequency and linguistic background

There was no correlation between the performance of respondents in the questionnaire and their fluency in English. Mother tongue speakers of English fared no better than respondents for whom English is a second or even a third language. In the case of the original version, the mother tongue of none of the respondents who provided the correct answers was English. In the case of the questionnaire based on the plain language version, only 30% of the respondents whose answers were correct were first language speakers of English. From this we may deduce that inaccessible legal language poses difficulties to readers regardless of their level of fluency in the language in which the text is written.[7]

---

7   In this regard, please see Chen, J "Law as a species of language acquisition" (1995) 73 *Washington University Law Quarterly* 1263; Bhatia, V K (1993) *Analysing Genre: Language use in professional settings*; Bowers, F (1989) *Linguistic aspects of legislative expression*; and Olson, D R, Torrance N & Hildyard, A (eds) (1985) *Literacy, language and learning*.

### 3.2.4 Correlation between correct response frequency and educational background

Once again there was very little correlation between the level of education and the correct response frequency. A slightly higher percentage of persons who have a tertiary education qualification was able to answer the original version, while both groups coped well with the plain language version.

### 3.3  Conclusion

Questionnaires based on the plain language version of the Act elicited the most accurate responses, arrived at within the shortest period of time. This indicates that texts drafted in plain language are more accessible than those drafted in legal language. The simplification of the overall structure of the text was therefore more beneficial for the comprehensibility of the Act than a mere simplification of the language.

Educational background, however, does play a role. Those respondents with a lower level of education coped less well with the original version of the text. This is significant as it is safe to assume that it will be those persons who have a lower level of formal education, thus belonging to a lower socio-economic sphere, who will least be able to afford a lawyer to "interpret" incomprehensible legal language.

There was no correlation between race, gender, age and profession, and the level of correct responses to the different versions.

In this study, linguistic background did not seem to play a significant role in the comprehensibility of the text.

## 4  Recommendations

In South Africa lawyers do not undergo formal training to qualify as judges. The theory is that their experience as lawyers makes them suitable to become judges.

However, writing a judgment is a skill. Years of practising law do not necessarily imply that one is able to write a good judgment.

When newly appointed judges underwent a brief training course in 1998, retired Chief Justice Corbett talked to them about writing a judgment.[8] He emphasised the problems posed by a heavy workload and the need to prevent delay. A consequence of this is that judges often give judgments orally. He continued: "To do so entails the judge being exceptionally articulate, being able to express himself orally with the same economy and facility of language as he can on paper."[9]

He asked the important question about who the intended audience of a judgment should be. He provided the following answer during an earlier interview: "Principally the parties, because they must understand why the judgment went the way it did."[10]

Bearing this in mind, he highlighted the importance of lucidity, orderliness, a logical structure and clear presentation. In short, he emphasised that judgments have to be readable. He gave the following practical guidelines: "Write in clear and simple language. Write clear and simple sentences. Write short sentences. Use headings to mark portions of the judgments."[11]

Amending the previous Chief Justice's guidelines slightly, we propose that the legal profession heed the following structure to facilitate clear and readable judgments (this includes judgments in magistrates' courts):

- The parties (Who are they?)
- Events resulting in the case being in this court (if this is at all relevant or important) (How did the parties come to be here?)
- Relief asked for (What do they want?)
- Legal issues (What should the judge decide about?)
- Facts (What is this dispute about, phrased in clear, concise language?)
- Applicable law (without too much authority, citation and footnotes) (What are the legal principles necessary to decide this case?)
- Application of law to facts (The judge applies the legal principles to the facts to answer the question and resolve the issue in a rational/motivated way.)
- Order (Do the parties get what they want?)
- Costs (Who pays for all this?)

---

8   Corbett, M M "Writing a judgment" (1998) 15 *South African Law Journal* 116.
9   Corbett, above, 119.
10  Nienaber, P M "Producing a judgment in the Appellate Division – an abridged and edited interview of an unreleased taped conversation which took place on 1 December 1993 between Chief Justice M M Corbett and one of his colleagues, Mr Justice Nienaber" in Kahn, E (ed) *The quest for justice* (1995) 285, 298.
11  Corbett, above, 125–126.

We propose the following to improve the drafting of legislation:
- Attempts to simplify texts should concentrate on the structure of those texts. Texts should be presented in such a way that structure aids comprehension.
- It may be useful to employ the skills of a layout specialist to identify the lay-out of a particular legislative text that would most successfully promote comprehension.
- It is important to note that it is not only second language speakers who struggle with incomprehensible legal language. Legalese is equally incomprehensible to mother tongue speakers of English.
- Training programmes in plain legal language should be introduced for drafters of legislation. These programmes should stress clarity.
- Before newly drafted legislative texts are used or promulgated, they should be tested on sample groups or readers to make sure that they are comprehensible.
- Information programmes will have to be organised to convince drafters of legislative texts of the necessity of implementing reform.

## APPENDIX A: QUESTIONNAIRE

SECTION A: BIOGRAPHICAL DATA
Please mark the applicable block with a cross (X) to describe yourself in respect of the following:

1.  Sex
    - ☐ Male
    - ☐ Female

2.  Age (years old)
    - ☐ below 20
    - ☐ 20 – 25
    - ☐ 26 – 35
    - ☐ 36 – 45
    - ☐ 46 – 55
    - ☐ 56 – 65
    - ☐ above 65
    - ☐ Other

3.  Race
    - ☐ Black
    - ☐ White
    - ☐ Coloured
    - ☐ Indian
    - ☐ Other

4.  Mother tongue
    - ☐ Sepedi
    - ☐ Setswana
    - ☐ Tshivenda
    - ☐ isiNdebele
    - ☐ Sesotho
    - ☐ Xitsonga
    - ☐ isiXhosa
    - ☐ Afrikaans
    - ☐ isiZulu
    - ☐ siSwati
    - ☐ English
    - ☐ Other

5.  Professional status
    - ☐ Practising lawyer
    - ☐ Judge/Magistrate
    - ☐ Legal academic

SECTION B: EVALUATION OF JUDGMENTS

1.  You have read judgments V and W. Which one do you like better? Please put a cross (X) next to the one you like better.
    - ☐ V
    - ☐ W

2. On a scale of 1 (very poor) to 10 (very good), how do you rate these two judgments?
   ❐ V
   ❐ W

3. **It you liked V better**, please give the two main reasons why you liked V better. Mark 1 next to your top reason and 2 next to your second top reason.
   ❐ It is more traditional.
   ❐ It uses familiar terminology.
   ❐ It gives the necessary details.
   ❐ Its formulations are more exact and precise.
   ❐ The other judgment leaves out important details.
   ❐ It cites more cases and legal rules than the other judgment.
   ❐ It is more convincing than the other judgment.
   ❐ The other judgment is too informal.
   ❐ Other reason: ...........................

   **OR**

   **If you liked judgment W better**, please give the two main reasons why you liked it better. Mark 1 next to your top reason and 2 next to your second top reason.
   ❐ It uses headings.
   ❐ It is better organised.
   ❐ It leaves out unnecessary detail.
   ❐ It is easier to read than the other judgment.
   ❐ It is shorter than the other judgment.
   ❐ It is less formal than the other judgment.
   ❐ It uses everyday language.
   ❐ Its arguments are clearer than that of the other judgment.
   ❐ Other reason: ...........................

4. Please read the following statements about the two judgments. In each instance, please circle the answer that gives the best assessment of your view.
   Key: Strongly agree (SA)
          Agree (A)
          Neutral (N)
          Disagree (D)
          Strongly disagree (SD)

   | | | |
   |---|---|---|
   | 4.1 | Judgment W is easy to understand. | SA  A  N  D  SD |
   | 4.2 | The writer of judgment V is a more educated person than the one who wrote judgment W. | SA  A  N  D  SD |
   | 4.3 | Judgment W is more scholarly than judgment V. | SA  A  N  D  SD |
   | 4.4 | Judgment V is easy to understand. | SA  A  N  D  SD |
   | 4.5 | Judgment V is more logical than judgment W. | SA  A  N  D  SD |

## APPENDIX B: JUDGMENT: THE VERSION REDRAFTED IN PLAIN LANGUAGE

*State v J*

### Background to the appeal
[1] A regional court found J guilty of attempted rape. He was sentenced to 18 months imprisonment in terms of the provisions of s 276(1)(i) of the Criminal Procedure Act 51 of 1977. He was sentenced to a further 18 months imprisonment, but this term of imprisonment was conditionally suspended for five years. He appealed unsuccessfully to the then Cape Provincial Division of the Supreme Court of South Africa against the regional court's decision. This appeal is now before us, after the trial court allowed the appeal.

### The complainant's version of events
[2] The complainant's evidence is the following: In the early hours of 26 December 1993, the complainant, a slightly built 17 year-old schoolgirl, accompanied by her sister, R, and some friends, set off to a park in Sydneyvale, Bishop Lavis in Cape Town to have some fun. They took a case of beer along. After a while J, a married and well-built 24 year old policeman, arrived at the scene in his car. He was known to the complainant. The atmosphere was merry and they drank the beer. The complainant had one beer. Later J offered to take some of the girls for a drive in his car, at the same time giving them driving lessons. The complainant, R and a friend, B, accepted the offer and off they went.

[3] After a while, R and B were dropped off in the park and J and the complainant drove to another nearby park in Sly Road. The complainant was driving the car. At this park J instructed the complainant to stop the car. When she asked why they had to stop, he replied that he wanted to finish the beer that he was drinking. She stopped the car and he drank a few glasses of beer.

[4] J tried to kiss her, but she turned away. He then told her that he had desired her for a long time. After that he grabbed both her hands and, with one of his hands, raised

them above her head. He overpowered her and took off his shoes. He lowered her jeans and panties to her ankles. Having succeeded in removing one leg of her jeans completely, he lowered the driving seat on which she was sitting, and heaved himself upon her. She tried to fight him off and eventually they ended up on the back seat of the car. She started shouting and screaming, but he put his hand over her mouth. She scratched him on the forehead. He then exposed his penis, forced her legs apart and tried to have intercourse. He also inserted a finger into her vagina. She pleaded with him, but he persisted in trying to force himself into her, still lying on top of her. She became hysterical, screaming and crying, and he stopped.

[5] She immediately jumped out of the car, pulled up her panties and jeans, and ran off, leaving her shoes in the car. She ran to a nearby house in search of help, but nobody opened the door. Two young men then approached her but, because she was terrified, she ran away. Eventually she ended up in the park where her sister and B were still enjoying themselves with friends. She was still hysterical and crying, and immediately told R that J had raped her.

[6] After a while J arrived at the park. The complainant accused J of having raped her, which he denied. R tried to assault J with a beer bottle and a friend removed the complainant's shoes from J's car. The police later found one of the complainant's earrings in the car. The complainant then proceeded to J's parents' home. There she also complained that J had raped her. Later that morning she and J were separately examined by the district surgeon.

**J's version of events**

[7] J denied that he raped, or attempted to rape, the complainant.

[8] J's version of events differs essentially from the complainant's. He said that they were talking in his car about intimate affairs. He kissed her, and she did not resist, but returned his attentions. They both moved to the passenger seat. He let down the passenger seat. She allowed

him to lie upon her. He started petting her breasts and private parts, while she remained fully clothed. She did not resist. After about two or three minutes things started "hotting up".

[9] Suddenly the complainant pushed him away, got out of the car and ran away. At no time did he expose his penis, take off her clothes, or put his finger into her vagina. J added that when the complainant accused him in the presence of R and others of having raped her, he denied having done so.

[10] When J was examined by the district surgeon, later that morning, scratch marks were found on his forehead and right ear. His explanation for this was that his wife had attacked him and scratched him on the forehead and ear when she heard of the complainant's accusations against him.

## Evidence confirming the complainant's version

[11] According to the evidence of the district-surgeon, the complainant was in a shocked and withdrawn condition when he saw her and she found the examination painful. He could not confirm that full penetration had taken place, but there were abrasions on her vaginal mucosa and buttocks, which are reconcilable with unlubricated sexual intercourse, but not readily reconcilable with J's version of what happened.

[12] The complainant's version was supported by R's evidence, at least in respect of the events before and after J's alleged misconduct. This evidence confirmed the following:
- The complainant had arrived at the park with her sister and friend.
- They had driven about with J and then returned to the park.
- The complainant and J had then driven off.
- She had later returned hysterical and barefoot, complaining that J had raped her.
- She had accused J of having raped her when he returned to the park.

[13] The complainant's mother testified that since the night in question the complainant had become withdrawn, had lost interest in her school work and had in effect dropped out of school.

## Finding by the regional magistrate

[14] The regional court magistrate rejected J's evidence as untrue and unreliable and accepted the complainant's version.

## Arguments before this court

[15] J's counsel argued that the trial court was making a mistake by not applying the cautionary rule in respect of the evidence of complainants in sexual cases. J's counsel argued that the magistrate was merely paying lip service to the rule.

[16] Counsel for the State denied this, but also argued that the basis, meaning and scope of the cautionary rule should be examined again. She argued that the rule, as it now applied in practice, was
- discriminatory towards women,
- unnecessary, and
- unfairly increased the burden of proof resting on the State in cases involving sexual offences.

## Question of law

[17] The question before this court is whether the application of the cautionary rule in all sexual offence cases is constitutional.

## The cautionary rule

[18] In *S v Snyman* 1968 (2) SA 582 (A) at 585C-H Judge of Appeal Holmes explained the cautionary rule as follows: Unlike an accomplice in a criminal trial, a complainant in a sexual case is *not ex hypothesi* criminal. Nevertheless in respect of both of them there exists an inherent danger in relying on their testimony. First, various motives may induce them to substitute the accused for the culprit. Second, from their participation in events which actually happened, each has a deceptive facility for convincing testimony, the only fiction being the deft substitution of the accused for the real culprit. Hence in sexual cases

there has grown up a cautionary rule of practice (similar to that in accomplice cases) which requires –
(a) the recognition by the Court of the inherent danger aforesaid; and
(b) the existence of some safeguard reducing the risk of wrong conviction, such as corroboration of the complainant in a respect implicating the accused, or the absence of gainsaying evidence from him, or his mendacity as a witness ...

Satisfaction of (a) and (b) will not per se warrant a conviction, for the ultimate requirement is proof beyond reasonable doubt; and this depends upon an appraisal of the totality of the evidence and the degree of safeguard aforesaid ... In this connection I respectfully agree with the observations of Macdonald AJP, in the Southern Rhodesian Appellate Division case of *R v J* 1966 (1) SA 88 at 90, to the effect that, while there is always need for special caution in scrutinising and weighing the evidence of young children, complainants in sexual cases, accomplices and, generally, the evidence of a single witness, the exercise of caution should not be allowed to displace the exercise of common sense.

### Evaluation of the basis of the rule

[19] The academic and legal literature on the history and justification of the rule is extensive and impressive. I have considered these contributions, but in view of the clear conclusions to which I have come, it is not necessary to review them in detail. I summarise my conclusions as follows:

[20] The idea that women often tend to lie about being raped, has existed for a long time. In our country, as in others, judges have attempted to justify the cautionary rule by relying on "collective wisdom and experience" (see the judgment of this Court in *S v Balhuber* 1987 (1) PH H22 (A) as discussed in *S v F* 1989 (3) SA 847 (A) at 853 et seq; 854F-855B). This was also the justification, before the reform of the law, in the UK. This justification lacks any factual or reality-based foundation, and can be exposed as a myth simply by asking: whose wisdom? whose experience? what proof is there of the assumptions underlying the rule?

### Empirical research

[21] The following empirical research disproves the idea that women lie more easily or frequently than men, or that they are intrinsically unreliable witnesses:
- An English Law Commission Working Paper (No 115) found no evidence to substantiate the cliché that the danger of false accusations is likely to exist merely because of the sexual character of the charge.
- The Supreme Court of California, in *P v Rincon-Pineda* (14 Cal 3d 864), despite a detailed examination of empirical data, found no evidence that complainants in sexual cases are more untruthful than complainants in other cases.
- The New York Sex Crimes Analysis Unit carefully analysed all allegations made to them over a period of two years. They found that the rate of false allegations for rape and sexual offences was around two percent. This rate was comparable with the rate for false complaints of other criminal offences (see DJ Birch, "Corroboration in Criminal Trials: A Review of the Proposals of the Law Commission's Working Paper", *Criminal Law Review* (1990) 667 at 678 note 69).

### Difficulties faced by rape victims

[22] The often quoted statement by Chief Justice Lord Hale in the seventeenth century that it is easy to bring a charge of rape (and difficult to disprove it) cannot be supported. Few things may be more difficult and humiliating for a woman than to cry rape:
- She is often, within certain communities, considered to have lost her credibility.
- She may be seen as unchaste and unworthy of respect.
- Her community may turn their back on her.
- She has to undergo the most harrowing cross-examination in court, where the intimate details of the crime are discussed repeatedly.
- She (but not the accused) may be required to reveal her previous sexual history.
- She may disqualify herself in the marriage market.
- Many husbands turn their backs on a "soiled" wife.

### Burden of proof may be affected

[23] It is also sometimes said that the rule does not affect the State's burden of proof. This is not correct. In *R v W* 1949 (3) SA 772 (A) Chief Justice Watermeyer at 783 said that had the case been one of theft, the evidence would have satisfied the test of proof beyond reasonable doubt. However, because the case was one of sexual assault, the same evidence would not be proof beyond reasonable doubt. In that case the accused was found not guilty because the case against him had not been proved beyond reasonable doubt although the trial court found strongly in favour of the truthfulness of the complainant and against that of the appellant.

### Comparative jurisdictions

[24] In comparable modern systems, the cautionary rule and its variations have been abolished in recent times. The following are examples:
- In Namibia, this was done by the judgment of Frank J in *S v D and Another*, above.
- In Canada s 8, chap 93 of the Criminal Law Amendment Act, 1974-75-76 did the same.
- In the UK, since s 32(1) of the Criminal Justice and Public Order Act, 1994 was adopted, courts no longer have to leave the cautionary rule in all cases.
- In New Zealand the rule was abolished by the Evidence Amendment Act (No 2) of 1985.
- S 62(3) of the Crimes Act abolished the rule in Australia.
- In California it was held in *P v Rincon-Pineda*, above, that the rule was groundless.

### Finding on question of law

[25] In my view, the cautionary rule in sexual assault cases is based on an irrational and outdated perception. It unjustly stereotypes complainants in sexual assault cases (overwhelmingly women) as particularly unreliable. In our system of law, the burden is on the State to prove the guilt of an accused beyond reasonable doubt – no more and no less. The evidence in a particular case may call for a cautionary approach, but that is a far cry from the application of a general cautionary rule.

**Application of cautionary rule**

[26] In formulating this approach to the cautionary rule under discussion I respectfully endorse the guidance provided by the Court of Appeal in *R v Makanjuola, R v Easton* [1995] 3 All ER 730 CA), a decision given after the legislative abrogation of the cautionary rule in England. Although the guidelines in that judgment were developed with a jury system in mind, the same approach, with the necessary changes by the context, is applicable to our law.

At 732f – 733a Chief Justice Lord Taylor stated:
> Given that the requirement of a corroboration direction is abrogated in the terms of s 32(1), we have been invited to give guidance as to the circumstances in which, as a matter of discretion, a judge ought in summing up to a jury to urge caution in regard to a particular witness and the terms in which that should be done. The circumstances and evidence in criminal cases are infinitely variable and it is impossible to categorise how a judge should deal with them. But it is clear that to carry on giving "discretionary" warnings generally and in the same terms as were previously obligatory would be contrary to the policy and purpose of the 1994 Act. Whether, as a matter of discretion, a judge should give any warning and if so its strength and terms must depend upon the content and manner of the witness's evidence, the circumstances of the case and the issues raised. The judge will often consider that no special warning is required at all. Where, however, the witness has been shown to be unreliable, he or she may consider it necessary to urge caution. In a more extreme case, if the witness is shown to have lied, to have made previous false complaints, or to bear the defendant some grudge, a stronger warning may be thought appropriate and the judge may suggest it would be wise to look for some supporting material before acting on the impugned witness's evidence. We stress that these observations are merely illustrative of some, not all, of the factors which judges may take into account in measuring where a witness stands in the scale of reliability and what response they should make at that level in their directions to the jury. We also stress that judges are not required to conform to any formula and this court would be slow to

interfere with the exercise of discretion by a trial judge who has the advantage of assessing the manner of a witness's evidence as well as its content.

[28] Lord Taylor then formulated eight guidelines, the third of which is particularly important for our purposes. It reads as follows (see at 733c-d):
(3) In some cases, it may be appropriate for the judge to warn the jury to exercise caution before acting upon the unsupported evidence of a witness. This will not be so simply because the witness is a complainant of a sexual offence nor will it necessarily be so because a witness is alleged to be an accomplice. There will need to be an evidential basis for suggesting that the evidence of the witness may be unreliable. An evidential basis does not include mere suggestions by cross-examining counsel.
(My emphasis.)

[29] The magistrate in the trial court was therefore not obliged to apply the rule.

**Application of law to facts**
[30] I am not convinced that the trial court made a mistake on the evidence before it, nor that the decision was wrong. On the contrary, the guilt of J was proved beyond reasonable doubt. The actions of the complainant were consistent with the allegations she had made. The abrasions found by the district-surgeon were compatible with her evidence and difficult to reconcile with J's version that he merely rubbed the complainant's private parts without using any force and while she was fully clad. His explanation of the scratches on his forehead and ear, uncorroborated as it was, would mean, if true, that the complainant was lying on this score. But how would she have known that he was injured, as it was never suggested that she was present when he was allegedly scratched by his wife?

[31] Furthermore, on both versions the complainant fled from the car, leaving her shoes there. This is incompatible with J's version of consensual and non-violent love-making. When the complainant reached her sister and friends, she was hysterical and immediately complained of having

been raped. The district-surgeon also reported that when he examined her, she was in a state of shock. This is incompatible with the J's version.

[32] There appears, from the evidence, to be no reason why the complainant would have lied to her sister and friends, to the district-surgeon, to the police and to the trial court. There were no bad feelings between the complainant and the accused before the incident occurred. On the contrary, they were driving around and he chose her to go with him for a further drive. He was a brother of her friend. There appears to be no reason for falsely implicating the accused in a serious crime and for bringing shame and hurt upon herself.

[33] In my view, the appeal against the conviction must fail.

**Appeal against sentence**
[34] If the sentence imposed by the trial court is open to criticism, it can only be that it sins on the side of leniency. The complainant was at the time a young slimly built schoolgirl. J was older, bigger and stronger. The evidence shows that she knew J was a policeman, and that she trusted him as a friend. His treatment of her was a despicable abuse of physical strength, and a violation of friendship and trust. The fact that he was a policeman whose duty it was to uphold law and order and not undermine it, is an aggravating factor. He acted in a manner unacceptable in our society. Our society is committed to the protection of the rights of all persons, including, especially, the right of women to their physical and moral integrity. Moreover, his actions had a serious damaging effect on the psyche of the complainant.

[35] There is no merit in the appeal against the sentence.

**Final result**
[36] The appeal against the conviction and sentence is therefore dismissed.

Mahomed C J, Van Heerden D C J, Streicher J A and Farlam A J A concurred. Appellant's Attorneys: Reuben Liddell, Wynberg; E G Cooper & Sons, Bloemfontein.

## APPENDIX C: ACTION FOR DIVORCE (ORIGINAL VERSION)

ACTION FOR DIVORCE IN TERMS OF ACT 70 OF 1979

1. The plaintiff is Maria Stevenson, an adult female.

2. The defendant is Jon Peter Stevenson, an adult male.

3. Plaintiff is ordinarily resident within the jurisdiction of this Honourable Court and has been ordinarily resident for a period of one year prior to the issue of summons in this action in the Republic of South Africa and she is domiciled within the said Republic.

4. The parties were married to each other at Johannesburg on 2 February 1991, which marriage still subsists.

5. (a) From the said marriage between the parties two children were born. Both are still minors and are presently in plaintiff's care.
   (b) It would be in the best interest of the children if the plaintiff were awarded custody and control of the children.

6. The marriage relationship between the parties has irretrievably broken down and there is no reasonable prospect of the restoration of a normal marriage relationship between them for the following reasons:
   (a) defendant has assaulted plaintiff repeatedly; and
   (b) the parties have not lived together as husband and wife for a period of more than one year.

WHEREFORE plaintiff claims:
(a) a decree of divorce;
(b) custody and control of the minor children born of the marriage;
(c) maintenance for the children in the amount of R800 per month per child;
(d) maintenance for plaintiff in the amount of R600 per month;
(e) a division of the joint estate.

## APPENDIX D: ACTION FOR DIVORCE (SIMPLIFIED VERSION)[12]

ACTION FOR DIVORCE IN TERMS OF ACT 70 OF 1979

1. The **plaintiff** is Maria Stevenson.

2. The **defendant** is Jon Peter Stevenson.

3. The plaintiff usually lived in the jurisdiction of this Court for one year before she issued a summons in this action.

4. The parties married in Johannesburg on 2 February 1991. They are still married.

5. (a) Two children were born from the marriage. Both children are minors and are in the plaintiff's care.
   (b) It would be in the best interest of the children to give their custody to the plaintiff.

6. The marriage between the parties has broken down beyond repair. It is very unlikely that a normal marriage relationship between them will be restored because
   - the defendant has assaulted the plaintiff many times, and
   - the parties have not lived together as a married couple for more than one year.

7. The plaintiff therefore claims:
   (a) An order of divorce.
   (b) Custody of the two children.
   (c) Maintenance for the children of R800 per month per child.
   (d) Maintenance for plaintiff of R600 per month.
   (e) A division of the joint estate.

---

12  This version is obviously also open to criticism. For example, in par 3 "usually lived" could have been replaced by "has lived", and "joint estate" in par 7 by "shared property".

**APPENDIX E:** THE BIRTHS AND DEATHS REGISTRATION ACT

1    Original version

Look at the following section from the Births and Deaths Registration Act 51 of 1992 and answer the question:
  11  (1) Any parent or guardian of a child born out of wedlock whose parents married each other after the registration of his or her birth, may, if such a child is a minor, or such child himself or herself may, if he or she is of age, apply to the Director-General to amend the registration of his or her birth and thereupon the Director-General shall, if satisfied that the applicant is competent to make the application, that the alleged parents of the child are in fact his or her parents and that they legally married each other, amend the registration of birth in such a manner as if such child's parents were legally married to each other at the time of his or her birth.

Sally Ackerman's school friends tease her because her surname is different from that of her father. She was born in 1985 when her mother, Sandra Ackerman, and father, Benny Benson, were living together. Because her mother was not married to her father at the time, Sally's birth was registered as "born out of wedlock" with the name Sally Ackerman. On 16 November 1995, however, Sally's parents married each other.

In 1996 Benny approaches the Department of Home Affairs with a request to change the registration of Sally's birth from "born out of wedlock" to "born inside wedlock".

Do you think it is possible to make this change? Refer to section 11 of the Births and Deaths Registration Act to explain your view.

2    Structure

Look at the following section from the Births and Deaths Registration Act 51 of 1992 and answer the following question:
  11  (1) (a) Any parent or guardian of a child born out of wedlock whose parents married each other after the registration of his or her birth, may, if such a child is a minor, apply to the Director-General to amend the

registration of his or her birth as if his or her parents were married to each other at the time of his or her birth.

(b) Any child born out of wedlock whose parents married each other after the registration of his or her birth, may, if he or she is of age, apply to the Director-General to amend the registration of his or her birth as if his or her parents were married to each other at the time of his or her birth.

(c) The Director-General shall amend the registration of birth in the prescribed manner as if such child's parents were married to each other if the Director-General is satisfied
   (i) that the applicant is competent to make the application,
   (ii) that the alleged parents of the child are in fact his or her parents, and
   (iii) that they legally married each other.

Sally Ackerman's school friends tease her because her surname is different from that of her father. She was born in 1985 when her mother, Sandra Ackerman, and her father, Benny Benson, were living together. Because her mother was not married to her father at the time, Sally's birth was registered as "born out of wedlock" with the name Sally Ackerman. On 16 November 1995, however, Sally's parents married each other.

In 1996 Benny approaches the Department of Home Affairs with a request to change the registration of Sally's birth from "born out of wedlock" to "born inside wedlock".

Do you think it is possible to make this change? Refer to section 11 of the Births and Deaths Registration Act to explain your view.

3    Language

Look at the following section from the Births and Deaths Registration Act 51 of 1992 and answer the following question:
   11 (1) A parent or guardian of a child who was born outside marriage whose parents married each other after the child's birth was formally registered may, if the child is a minor, or if the child is no longer a minor, the child

personally, may apply to the Director-General to change his or her birth registration as if his or her parents were married to each other when the child was born, and after that the Director-General must, if satisfied that the applicant is able to make the application and that the alleged parents of the child are really his or her parents, and that the parents are legally married to each other, change the registration of the birth in the prescribed way as if the parents had been legally married to each other when the child was born.

Sally Ackerman's school friends tease her because her surname is different from that of her father. She was born in 1985 when her mother, Sandra Ackerman, and father, Benny Benson, were living together. Because her mother was not married to her father at the time, Sally's birth was registered as "born out of wedlock" with the name Sally Ackerman. On 16 November 1995, however, Sally's parents married each other.

In 1996 Benny approaches the Department of Home Affairs with a request to change the registration of Sally's birth from "born out of wedlock" to "born inside wedlock".

Do you think it is possible to make this change? Refer to section 11 of the Births and Deaths Registration Act to explain your view.

4   Language and structure

Look at the following section from the Births and Deaths Registration Act 51 of 1992 and answer the following question:

11  (1) (a) A parent or guardian of a child who was born outside marriage whose parents married each other after the child was formally registered may, if the child is a minor, apply to the Director-General to change the birth registration as if his or her parents were married to each other when that child was born.

(b) A child who was born outside marriage whose parents married each other after that child's birth was formally registered may apply to the Director-General to change the birth registration as if his or her parents were married to each other when that child was born.

(c) The Director-General must change the birth registration in the prescribed way as if the child's parents had been legally married to each other when the child was born, if the Director-General is satisfied that
  (i) the applicant is able to make the application, and
  (ii) that the alleged parents of the child are really the child's parents, and
  (iii) that the parents legally married each other.

Sally Anderson's school friends tease her because her surname is different from that of her father. She was born in 1985 when her mother, Sandra Anderson, and father, Benny Benson, were living together. Because her mother was not married at the time, Sally's birth was registered as "born out of wedlock" with the name Sally Anderson. On 16 November 1995, however, Sally's parents married each other.

In 1996 Benny approaches the Department of Home Affairs with a request to change the registration of Sally's birth from "born out of wedlock" to "born inside wedlock".

Do you think it is possible to make this change? Refer to section 11 of the Births and Deaths Registration Act to explain your view.

## 5     Plain language version

Look at the following section from the Births and Deaths Registration Act 51 of 1992 and answer the following question:
  (a) If you are the parent or guardian of a child who was born before you married that child's father or mother, and your child is not yet 21 years old, you may ask the Director-General to change the registration of your child's birth so that it looks as if you were already married to your child's mother or father when your child was born.
  (b) If your parents only married each other after you were born, and you are older than 21, you may ask the Director-General to change your birth registration so that it looks as if your parents were already married to each other when you were born.
  (c) To change a birth registration in this way, the Director-General must be sure that
    (i) the person asking for the change has the right to ask for the change, and

(ii) the child's parents are really the child's parents, and
(iii) the parents legally married.

Sally Ackerman's school friends tease her because her surname is different from that of her father's. She was born in 1985 when her mother, Sandra Ackerman, and father, Benny Benson, were living together. Because her mother was not married to her father at the time, Sally's birth was registered as "born out of wedlock" with the name Sally Ackerman. On 16 November 1995, however, Sally's parents married each other.

In 1996 Benny approaches the Department of Home Affairs with a request to change the registration of Sally's birth from "born out of wedlock" to "born inside wedlock".

Do you think it is possible to make this change? Refer to section 11 of the Births and Deaths Registration Act to explain your view.

# F
# Conclusion

F.1 Conclusion — page 157
F.2 Launch of Clarity in
    South Africa — page 159

## F.1
# Conclusion

**Frans Viljoen**
Faculty of Law, University of Pretoria

**Annelize Nienaber**
Faculty of Law, University of Pretoria

We hope that the contributions in this book show the benefits of using plain language. The benefits of plain legal language (in tone, language, structure and design) are many, including better comprehension, savings in time and money, and greater accessibility of the law. The majority of South Africans are poor and relatively uneducated. Seen from their perspective, the South African legal system verges on being totally alienating and extremely remote because of the language that is used. The legitimacy of the legal system is under threat.

It has already been accepted to a certain extent that there is a need for plain legal language in South Africa. The conference has shown that members of government, lawyers and drafters support plain language. We mention some of the noteworthy responses in this book. To this the following may be added:
- Section 3(2)(a) of the Promotion of Administrative Justice Act[1] provides that fairness in administrative procedures depends on a number of factors. One of these factors is "a clear statement of the administrative action".
- The combined judgment of Ackermann J, O'Regan J and Sachs J in *Prinsloo v Van der Linde*[2] is an example of the Constitutional Court's approach to clearer structure and simpler language. This does not mean that such language

---
1  3 of 2000.
2  1997 3 SA 1012 (CC) par 1.

needs to be dull. Read the first few sentences of the judgment, dealing with a relatively unexciting subject, the prevention of veld fires:

> Much of South Africa is tinder dry. Veld, forest and mountain fires sweep across the land, causing immense damage to property and destroying valuable forest, flora and fauna. The Forest Act has as one of its principal objects the prevention and control of such fires.

The question arises: What is the best strategy to "mainstream" plain legal language?

Participants at the conference divided into workshop groups and discussed the following possibilities:
- Should the government adopt a centralised Plain Language Act?
- Should provisions imposing plain language obligations be inserted into particular statutes?

The first possibility is a comprehensive Plain Language Act. The main provision of a Plain Language Act should state that "legal documents must be written in as understandable language as the subject matter allows" and must be "designed in a way that helps readers understand the document". The obligation to comply will differ, depending on the nature of the legal document (for example legislation, by-laws or a contract). Such an Act will bind both government (at all levels) and private practitioners.

Courts should be able to order appropriate remedies. In this regard, Elliot[3] proposes fines. For every use of "said", for example, a transgressor must pay $75 to a Plain Language Institute. There is a schedule to his proposed Plain Language Act which stipulates fines. He also proposes that courts order that drafters rewrite documents.

Workshop participants decided against the introduction of a Plain Language Act, at least at this stage. The dominant view was that focus should fall on raising awareness and on changing attitudes. We hope this publication will be one step in this direction, and will help realise the goal implicit in the words of our previous Chief Justice:[4]

> There is no reason why the law should be, and remain, an occult science understood only by lawyers. In fact society's distrust of lawyers and the law is mainly due to the tendency of lawyers in the past to keep the law to themselves.

---

3    (1993) 27 *Clarity* 13.
4    Corbett, MM "Writing a judgment" (1998) 115 *South African Law Journal* 116 at 122.

## F.2
# Launch of Clarity in South Africa

**Mark Adler**
*Chairman, Clarity*

In 1983 the *Gazette* of the English Law Society published a letter from a surveyor complaining that the traditional style of lease drafting caused enormous problems for those, like him, who had to interpret them as part of their daily routine. This prompted a letter in the next issue from John Walton, a local authority solicitor, inviting anyone interested in forming a group to promote plain legal language to write to him with a £5 subscription. So Clarity was born.

We now have just over 1 000 members and are represented in nearly 30 countries. Most of our members are practising lawyers, from sole practitioners in the High Street to partners in what is about to become the largest firm in the world. Our members include solicitors, barristers, attorneys, judges (including the Lord Chief Justice of England), national and local government lawyers (including parliamentary counsel from many jurisdictions), academics, law libraries (which have joined for the subscription to the journal rather than as members in the normal sense), and legal translators.

We have never had a constitution. We found that the group worked without one so decided to live by our principle that unnecessary verbiage should be avoided. Everything about the group is informal. No one proposes or seconds motions at meetings; if someone has a proposal they just suggest it.

If someone wants help they ask and (within reason) we try to give it. I am always happy to put people in touch with members with particular expertise or in a particular geographical area, so far as I can from the information on my database. (They may of course be asked to pay the member for professional services as opposed to informal advice.)

The annual subscription has for some years now been £15, the increase having been necessary to fund the printing and distribution of our journal, which comes out rather erratically, I am afraid, but as close to every six months as we can manage. Between issues we publish a single-sheet newsletter, and meanwhile post news on our website.

We now have local representatives in the USA, Canada, Australia, Singapore, and Hong Kong. Frans Viljoen has kindly agreed to be our representative in South Africa. The idea is that he recruits members and collects the subscriptions in local currency, to avoid the disproportionate bank charges if you send £15 to England. He takes his expenses and once a year passes any surplus to our treasurer in England. The journals and newsletters are posted direct from England. And if the local group wants to run its own activities, so much the better.

If you are at this conference you are probably sympathetic to our aims and I hope you will all join. I have brought copies of our journal for everyone and there is an application form on the back page (intended to be photocopied rather than torn off).

More information (including, for example, a plain language book list) can be obtained from our website at: www.adler.demon.co.uk/clarity.htm.

# G
# Plain language sources

G.1 General sources — page 163
G.2 Sources with a South African focus — page167
G.3 General webpages — page169
G.4 Webpages of South African interest — page169

## G.1
## General sources

Adler, M *Clarity for lawyers* (1990) London: The Law Society

Aiken, R J "Let's not oversimplify legal language" (1960) 32 *University of Colorado Law Review* 358

Asprey, M M *Plain language for lawyers* 2nd ed (1996) Sydney: The Federation Press

Bailey, E P *Writing clearly* (1984) Columbus, Ohio: Merrill

Balmford, C "Adding value by writing clearly" (1994) 3 *The South African Law Journal* 514

Benson, R W "The end of legalese: The game is over" (1985) XIII *Review of Law and Social Change* 519

Benson, R W "Up a statute with a gun and a camera: Isolating linguistic and logical structures in the analysis of legislative language" (1984) 8 *Seton Hall Legislative Journal* 279

Benson, R W and Kessler, J B "Legalese v Plain English: An empirical study of persuasion and credibility in appellate brief writing" (1987) 20 *Loyola of Los Angeles Law Review* 301

Bhatia, V K *Analysing genre: Language use in professional settings* (1993) Essex: Longman

Bowers, F *Linguistic aspects of legislative expression* (1989) Vancouver: University of British Columbia Press

Bowers, F *Linguistic aspects of legislative expression* (1989) Vancouver: University of British Columbia Press

Bransford, R et al "Sentence memory: A constructive versus interpretive approach" (1972) *Cognitive Pschology* 193–209

Butt, P "Plain language in conveyancing?" (November 1992) 66 *Australian Law Journal* 741

Chen, J "Law as a species of language acquisition" (1995) 73 *Washington University Law Quarterly* 1263

*Clarity* – 1983 – 2000 (Newsletter of *Clarity*, a movement to simplify legal languagea)

Cutler-Stuart, M *How to write essays* (1985) Sydney: Hale & Iremonger

Cutts, M & Maher, C *Gobbledygook* (1984) London: George Allen & Unwin

Cutts, M & Maher, C *The plain English story* (1986) Stockport, UK: Plain English Campaign

Cutts, M *Lucid Law* (1994) Stockport, UK: Plain English Campaign

Cutts, M *Making sense of English in law* (1992) Edinburg & New York: Chambers

Cutts, M (1995) *The plain English guide* New York: Oxford University Press

Danet, B "Language in the legal process" (1980) 14 *Law & Society Review* 445

Darville, R & Reid, G *Guidelines for writing, editing and designing* (1985) Ottawa: Canadian Law Information Council

Davison, A & Green, GM (eds) *Linguistic complexity and text comprehension: Readability issues reconsidered* (1988) New Jersey: Lawrence Erlbaum Associates

Eagleson, R D "Efficiency in legal drafting" (1988) *Adelaide Law Review* 13–27

Eagleson, R D "Informed consent: A linguistic perspective" in Waller, L (ed) *Medicine, science and the law: Informed consent* (1986) Melbourne: Law Reform Commission of Victoria 23–43

Eagleson, R D *Plain English in official writing* (1985) Canberra: Department of Administrative Services, Information Coordination Branch (Plain English and Simpler Forms Programme)

Eagleson, R D *The case for plain English* (1983) Canberra: Department of Administrative Services, Information Coordination Branch (Plain English and Simpler Forms Programme)

Eagleson, R D *The reform of documents within government departments in the United Kingdom* (1983) Canberra: Department of Administrative Services, Information Coordination Branch (Plain English and Simpler Forms Programme)

Eagleson, R D *Writing in plain English* (1990) Canberra: Australian Government Publishing Service

Edgerton, T S "In disgust of legalese" (December 1986) 66 *Michigan Bar Journal* 306

Edgerton, T S "The Ten Commandments of how to not write in Plain English (otherwise known as the Elements of Legalese)" (November 1986) 65 *Michigan Bar Journal* 1168

Felker, B D & others *Guidelines for document designers* (1981) American Institute for Research

Felker, D B (ed) *Document design: A review of relevant research* (1980) Washington DC: Document Design Center

Flesch, R *How to write plain English: A book for lawyers and consumers* (1979) New York: Harper & Row

Garner, B (ed) *The Scribes Journal of Legal Writing* Texas: West Publishing Company (1990)

Garner, B *Dictionary of modern legal usage* 2nd ed (1995) Oxford: Oxford University Press

Garner, B *Guidelines for drafting and editing court rules* (1996) Administrative Office of the US Courts

Garner, B *The elements of legal style* (1991) Oxford: Oxford University Press

Gibbs, H "Judgment writing" (1993) 67 *Australian Law Journal* 494

Gowers, E *The complete plain words* 3rd ed Greenbaum, S & Whitcut, J (1986) London: Her Majesty's Stationery Office

Horowitz, R & Samuels, S J (eds) *Comprehending oral and written language* (1987) San Diego: Academia Press

Kimble, J "Writing for dollars, writing to please" (1996–1997) 6 *The Scribes Journal of Legal Writing,* especially 24–25

Kimble, J "Answering the critics of plain language" (1994–1995) 5 *The Scribes Journal of Legal Writing* 51

Kimble, J "Plain English: A charter for clear writing" (1992) 9 *Thomas M Cooley Law Review* 1

Kimble, J "The many uses of 'shall' " (1992) 3 *The Scribes Journal of Legal Writing* 61

Law Reform Commission of Victoria *Plain English and the law* (manual for legislative drafters) (manual for legislative drafters) (1987) Melbourne: Victoria Government Printer

McKillop, B "What lawyers think about plain legal language" (1994) *Law Society Journal* 68–69

Mellinkoff, D *The language of the law* (1963) Boston: Little, Brown & Company

Murphy, E M *Effective writing: Plain English at work* (1989) Melbourne: Pitman Publishing

Nolta, J V *Taal in toga* (1997) Deventer: Kluwer

Olson, D R, Torrance N & Hildyard, A (eds) *Literacy, language and learning* (1985) Cambridge: Cambridge University Press

Plain English Campaign *Language on trial* (1995) London: Robson Books
Plain English Campaign *Utter drivel* (1995) London: Robson Books
Prutting, E "Pragmatics as social competence" (1982) *Journal of Speech and Hearing Disorders* 25

Redish, J C *How to write regulations and other legal documents in clear English* (1991) Washington DC: American Institutes for Research, Document Design Center
Redish, J C *The language of the bureaucracy* (1981) Washington DC: Document Design Center

Semegen, P W "Plain language legislation" (1980) Jan-Feb *Case & Comment* 42
Shieber, P H "Goodbye to leglaese: New plain language law spells good news for consumers" (July 1993) 16 *Pennsylvania Law Journal* 5
*Simply stated* (Newsletter of the Document Design Centre) Washington (1979)
Strunk, W Jr & White, E B *The elements of style* 3rd ed (1979) New York: Macmillan
Swales, J M & Bhatia, V K "An approach to the linguistic study of legal documents" (1983) 83 *Fachsprache* 98

Thomas, M *A clear guide to chaos: A practitioner's guide to wills* (1992) London: Fourmat Publishing
Turk, C & Kirkman, J *Effective writing* (1982) London: E & FN Spon

Vernon, T *Gobbledegook* (1980) London: National Consumer Council

Walsh, B *Communicating in writing* 2nd ed (1989) Canberra: AGPS Press
Wilson, C A *Plain language pleadings* (1996) New Jersey: Prentice Hall
Wydick, R C *Plain English for lawyers* 3rd ed (1985) Durham NC: Carolina Academic Press

## G.2
# Sources with a South African focus

Du Toit, D C "Suksesvolle regstaal" (1978) 124 *De Rebus* 187

Du Toit, D C "Suksesvolle regstaal" (1979) 136 *De Rebus* 223

Fine, D *How to use plain language* (1995) Cape Town Legal Education Action Project (LEAP)

Gentle, R *Plain language in prospectuses: What we can learn from the US* (1998) Johannesburg: Plain Business Writing

Gentle, R *Short, persuasive letters* (1998) Johannesburg: Plain Business Writing

Gentle, R *Short, punchy reports* (1998) Johannesburg: Plain Business Writing

Gentle, R *The basics of short, plain language* (1988) Johannesburg: Plain Business Writing

Gutto, S "Plain language and the law in the context of cultural and legal pluralism" (1995) 11 *South African Journal on Human Rights* 311

Hiemstra, V G "Afrikaans as regstaal" (1975) 16 *Codicillus* 4

James, P "Drafters of South Africa's new constitution adapt to plain language" (1997) 38 *Clarity* 13

Kahn, E "The Plain English Movement and accessibility to the law" (1992) 9 *The English Academy Review* 83

Kimble, J & Balmford, C "Plain language takes off in South Africa" (1995) 33 *Clarity* 8

Kleyn, D & Viljoen, F *Beginner's guide for law students* (Chapter 17) (1998) Cape Town: Juta

Knight, P "CLARITY in South Africa" (1996) 34 *Clarity* 20

Knight, P "Clearly better drafting: Testing two versions of the South African Human Rights Commission Act, 1995" (1997) 38 *Clarity* 8

Nienaber, A G "The accessibility and comprehensibility of South Africa's Bill of Rights: An empirical study" (2001) 1 *De Jure* 113

Nienaber, A G & Van der Walt, C "The language needs of undergraduate law students: An empirical investigation" (1996) 1 *De Jure* 71

Omar, D "Plain language, the law and the right to information" (1995) 33 *Clarity* 11

Stewart-Smith, A "The legislated bluff: How democratic rights are undermined by the language of the new constitution in South Africa" (1996) 34 *Clarity* 15

Van der Walt, C & Nienaber, A G *English for law students* (Unit 9) (1997) Cape Town: Juta

Van der Westhuizen, J V "Opmerkings in verband met taal en die reg" in Pretorius, R (ed) *Taal en beroep* (1986) Pretoria: University of Pretoria, Faculty of Arts

Viljoen, F "Die storie van Afrikaans as regstaal" (1992) *De Jure* 439

Viljoen, F "Pleidooi vir eenvoudiger en juister regstaal" (1998) 61 *Tydskrif vir Hedendaagse Romeins-Hollandse Reg* 714

## G.3
# General webpages

<http://www.cba.org/abc/LawyersForLiteracy> (a kit about how to adapt office practice to the needs of clients with low literacy levels)

<http://www.sec.gov/news/plaineng.htm> (includes the SEC *Plain English Handbook*)

<http://www.demon.co.uk/plainenglish> (Plain English Campaign)

<http://www.lawlink.nsw.gov.au> (New South Wales Attorney General's site – has links to court information, fair trading, dealing with crime, rights at work, victims of crime, privacy, people with disabilities)

<http://www.lawsoc.asn.au> (information sheets on a range of issues including wills, families, courts, using a lawyer)

<http://www.law4u.com.au> (plain English legal information)

<http://www.rlc.org.au> (Redfern Centre – tenancy, credit and debt fact sheet)

<http://www.adler.demon.co.uk/eng.htm> (Adler & Adler, *Clarity*)

<http://www.faa.gov/language> (US Federal Aviation Authority)

<http://www.plainlanguage.gov> (US government plain language)

## G.4
# Webpages of South African interest

<http://www.plainwriting.co.za> (plain business writing)
<http://www.up.ac.za/chr> (plain legal language)

# Contributors

H

# Contributors

### Adler, Mark
Mark Adler has always lived in England. He graduated in Philosophy from Warwick University in 1971, obtained a teaching certificate the following year, and taught briefly in a primary school in London before joining his father as an articled clerk in 1972. He stayed on after he had qualified as a solicitor in 1979 and inherited the practice on this father's death in 1980. He is chairman of Clarity – an international movement for plain legal language – and has edited its journal since 1987. He is the author of *Clarity for Lawyers* (the English Law Society's book on plain legal language) and of many articles. He teaches plain legal writing in the UK and overseas, and helps other lawyers improve their own and clients' documents.

### Alberts, Mariëtta
Dr Alberts started her career as a terminologist at the Terminology Bureau of the Department of National Education.

After 10 years as a terminologist she went to the Human Sciences Research Council (HSRC) to do research into terminology, lexicography and computational linguistics. At the HSRC she was a member of the interdisciplinary LEXINET research team. She spearheaded the development of a computer program (called LEXI) for the documentation of lexicographical data.

In 1995 she rejoined the National Terminology Services (previously known as Terminology Bureau); (now Terminology and Place Names of the National Language Service, Department of Arts, Culture, Science and Technology) as Head: Systems Development & Research.

She is a member of the Suid-Afrikaanse Akademie vir Wetenskap en Kuns (SAAWK).

She is a council member of the International Organisation for Unification of Terminological Neologisms (IOUTN) and assists with an international research project for the compilation of a multilingual dictionary of international terms of the World Bank of International Terms (WBIT) within IOUTN.

She is also a founder member of the Centre for Legal Terminology in African Language (CLTAL) and acts as its secretary. She teaches Lexicography to postgraduate students on a part-time basis at the Department of African Languages, University of Pretoria.

## Armstrong, Amanda

Amanda is a partner at Cheadle, Thompson & Haysom, Johannesburg.

During 1994–1995 she campaigned for and was involved in drafting the new Labour Relations Act in plain language.

In November 1996 she attended a conference in Auckland, New Zealand, on drafting tax legislation in plain language. She met with international experts on plain language and the law. She wrote an article reviewing the conference which was published in an international plain language journal, *Clarity*. Subsequent to the conference she went to Sydney and met with lawyers heading plain language departments in two of the leading Australian law firms, namely Phillips Fox and Mallesons Stephens Jacques.

In 1997 she was involved in drafting the Employment Equity Bill in plain language and in 1998 she was involved in drafting the Electoral Bill in plain language. She undertakes ongoing plain language work for the government, non-governmental organisations, trade unions and commercial clients.

She is presently responsible for ensuring that plain language is both a feature and a product of the service provided by the law firm Cheadle, Thompson & Haysom. She is working with leading Canadian and Australian experts in this regard.

## Daniels, Enver

Enver Daniels is the Chief State Law Adviser.

## Fine, Derrick

Derrick is a legally qualified training, plain language and research consultant, based in Cape Town. Derrick has 20 years of experience of working in human rights organisations, a human rights law firm, the Legal Education Action Project, the Constitutional Assembly and more recently, as a freelance consultant.

Derrick's areas of specialisation include the following:
- developing human rights, paralegal and community education materials

- plain language writing, editing and revision of documents and materials in the legal, medical and environmental disciplines
- plain language and effective communication skills training

Derrick has designed and facilitated plain language, legal and paralegal skills training programmes in South Africa, Namibia, Zimbabwe, Malawi, Kenya, Uganda, Ethiopia, Gambia and Palestine.

### Leppan, Chris

Chris holds the degrees BA LLB (Rhodes) and HDipTax (Wits). He is an attorney and for the past 10 years he has been Group Legal Adviser for WesBank, a Division of FirstRand Bank Ltd. At WesBank he specialises in all facets of asset-based financing, joint finance companies and other corporate structures. He has been the chairman of the Asset-Based Finance Association (previously the Association of General Banks) for the past four years.

### Omar, Dullah

Minister Omar was appointed to the Cabinet of President Nelson Mandela as Minister of Justice, and to that of President Mbeki as Minister of Transport. He practised as an attorney.

### Van der Westhuizen, Johann

Judge Johann van der Westhuizen was born on 26 May 1952 in Windhoek. In 1973 and 1975 he was awarded the BA (Law) and LLB degrees respectively. He obtained both these degrees with distinction at the University of Pretoria. As a student, he received several academic prizes and awards, including the Grotius-penning from the Pretoria Bar as the best final-year student in the LLB course. In 1980 he obtained his doctorate with a thesis entitled *Noodtoestand as regsverdigingsgrond in die strafreg*.

In 1976, he was appointed a senior lecturer in the Department of Legal History and Jurisprudence at the University of Pretoria, and in 1980 he was promoted to professor and later to head of the department.

After the establishment of the Centre for Human Rights at the University of Pretoria in 1986, he became its first director. He became involved in numerous human rights-related activities, including the drafting of the Interim Constitution. In 1996 he was appointed as one of the constitutional experts to advise the Constitutional Assembly on the drafting of the final Constitution. Thereafter he headed a task team to draft equality legislation for South Africa.

He is an advocate of the High Court. In 1998 he acted as judge of the High Court, and in 1999 he was appointed permanently to this bench.

He is also the author of numerous articles.


### Viljoen, Frans and Nienaber, Annelize

Frans Viljoen and Annelize Nienaber are both lecturers in the Faculty of Law, University of Pretoria. They are involved in teaching introductory courses for first-year law students, as well as Human Rights, and Law and Literature. Both Frans and Annelize hold degrees in law as well as in language: Frans an MA in Afrikaans, and Annelize a BA(Hons) in English. Both are co-authors of a textbook for first-year law students: Frans the *Beginner's Guide for Law Students*, and Annelize *English for Law Students*. Frans previously worked as a public prosecutor and state advocate, and Annelize lectured at Vista University. They have conducted an empirical research project on plain legal language.

# INDEX

Afrikaans 9–10, 13, 25, 59, 67, 94, 97, 99–101, 107, 109, 112–113, 116, 121, 129, 136, 167, 176
Accessibility of legal language, empirical research project 13, 121, 129, 176
Action for divorce, original version 126, 148
Action for divorce, simplified version 126, 149
Adler, Mark 12–13, 36, 173
African languages
    Ndebele 113, 136
    Nguni languages 109, 114
    Sepedi 93–94, 96, 100–103, 106–107, 109, 113–114, 136
    Sesotho 93, 108–109, 113–114, 136
    Setswana 109, 114, 136
    Siswati 93, 113, 136
    Sotho languages 93, 108–109, 113–114, 136
    Tsonga 99, 113, 136
    Tswana 109, 112–114, 136
    Venda 99, 113, 136
    Xhosa 59, 113–114
    Zulu 59, 113, 136
Arbitration Act (UK) 39
Attitude to different versions (original and plain language), dependent on age 133
    educational level 20, 128
    gender 26, 133, 127
    legal profession (membership of) 32, 37, 94, 122, 124, 128
    profession 32, 37, 122, 124, 128
    race 125, 133
    years in legal profession 124, 128
Australia, plain language in 31–35, 38, 144

Balmford, Christopher 10
Basic Conditions of Employment Act (75 of 1997) 85
Benefits of plain language 22, 25, 32, 157
Bibliography 89, 116
Bill of Rights 58, 65, 67, 70
Births and Deaths Registration Act (51 of 1992) 129, 150–154

Brittain, plain language in
    commerce 38, 79
    current developments 13, 36
    degrees of plainness 23–24
    law firms and the bar 34
    local government 34, 44
    statutes 11, 38

Canada, plain language in 29
Centre for Legal Terminology in African Languages (CLTAL) 89, 93–94
Centre for Plain Legal Language (Australia) 32
Centre for Science Development (HSRC) 121, 173
Civil Procedure Rules (UK) 42
Clarity awards 43
*Clarity* (journal) 13, 30, 36, 38, 174
Clarity (organisation) 12, 15, 37, 39, 44
Clinton, President (USA) 47, 49
Common law 98–99, 104
Communication Research Institute 32
Conference and workshop (of 2 July 1999)
    conference aim 12
    conference participants 12–13
    conference programme 13–14
Connotation 103
Constitution
    1993 (interim) constitution 10, 64, 66–67, 176
    1996 (final) constitution 11, 61, 66, 176
    cross-references 69–70, 74
    drafting of 61, 64–65, 176
    section 10 (final constitution) 66
    section 10 (interim constitution) 66
    section 12 (interim constitution) 67
    section 13 (final constitution) 67
    section 13 (interim constitution) 68
    section 14 (final constitution) 68
    section 174 (3) (final constitution) 69
    section 97(2)(a) (interim constitution) 68
    use of "shall" 66–67
Constitutional Assembly 11, 61, 63–65, 174, 176
Constitutional Court 12, 68–69, 157

Corbett, Chief Justice 133
Cross-reference 69–70, 74
Cutts, Martin 37, 81
Culture specific nature of terms 96

Democracy, plain language and 10, 57–58
Department of Arts, Culture, Science and Technology 109, 173
Department of Justice 60, 65
Department of Labour 72, 75
Document Design Center (USA) 166
Drafting 11, 13, 25, 32, 37–38, 42, 56, 62, 64–66, 69–71, 75, 78–79, 83–85, 174, 176

Embedding 103
Empirical research 121, 143
Employment Equity Act (55 of 1998) 85
English Law Society 173
European Union 30, 111
Executive order 12866 (1993) (President Clinton memorandum (1999)) 32, 47

Faculty of Law, University of Sydney 32
Federal Aviation Authority (USA) 50
Federal administrative regulations 47
Footnotes, use of 66, 75, 134
Foreign words
　Latin 36, 88, 102, 105
　French 36, 96, 102, 111

Garner, Bryan 51
Gender 26, 133, 127
*Guidelines for Document Designers* (USA) 164
Guidelines for plain language 56, 85
*Guinness Book of Records* 55
Gutto, Shadrack 10, 14

Harmonisation 92, 108, 109–110, 112–114
Human Sciences Research Council (HSRC) 121, 173

Illiteracy 79
Income tax law, rewriting of Australia's 33

Indigenous languages 92, 100, 112 *see* African languages
Information, right to 55, 58–60
International 10, 11, 13, 27, 95, 110, 173–174
International Organisation for Unification of Terminological Neologisms (IOUTN) 110, 118, 173
Internationalisation 110–112, 114

Judgments, plain language in 85, 134
Judgment: *S v Jackson* – redrafted version 122

Kimble, Joe 10, 51
Knight, Phil 10

Labour Relations Act (LRA) (66 of 1995)
　design and layout 32, 71, 75, 174
　drafting in plain language 13, 15, 71, 174
　excerpts as illustration 71, 76
　ripple-effects of plain language drafting 71, 75
　sentence structure and language 71, 74, 174
　structure 71–74, 174
Language for Special Purposes (LSP) 90
Language Plan Task Group (Langtag) 91
Latin *see* Foreign words
Law Foundation of New South Wales 15, 32
Law Reform Commission of Victoria 32, 84
Leases, plain language 14, 34, 46, 86
Legal language (legalese) 12–13, 21–22, 34, 36–37, 42, 53, 61, 68, 89–91, 115, 121–122, 124, 126–128, 132–133, 135, 159
Legal terminology, multilingual 89, 92, 97, 104
Legislation, in plain language 32–34, 46, 79
　Labour Relations Act (66 of 1995) 71
　Mine Health and Safety Act (29 of 1996) 11
Legislative incentives in Australia 33
Legislative process 83
*Lingua franca* 91

Literacy 20, 25, 59, 81, 92
Loan words 100, 102

Mason, Anton 31
"May" 67, 75
Mellinkoff, David 36
Multilingualism, plain language and 14, 89, 91, 97, 104, 109
"Must" 11, 75

Namibian Constitution 53
National Research Foundation (NRF) 15, 121
National Water Act, 1998 85
Neologisms 102–103, 110–111, 113
*New South Wales Law Society Journal* 32
New Zealand 29, 144, 174

Occupational Safety and Health Administration 47
Office of Fair Trading 38
Omar, Dullah, address by 15, 55

Pan-South African Language Board (PANSALB) 94
Parliament 39, 62, 65, 67, 70, 78, 80, 85, 102
Passive 24, 43, 68, 70, 74, 84
Plain Business Writing 12, 14
Plain English Campaign 11, 37
*Plain English Handbook* (USA) 47
Plain Language Act (New Jersey) 46, 158
Plain Language, barriers to
    cost 20
    attitudes 20
    language diversity 20 *see also* multilingualism
    educational level 20
    difficulty of legal language 20
Plain language communication 13, 15, 19–20, 25
Plain Language Committees and Plain Language Units 33
Plain language approach, features of
    flow diagram 75, 77
    language (understandable) 59, 71, 75, 129, 134, 152, 158
    lay-out and design 71, 75, 81, 135, 157
    "must" replacing "shall" 11, 67
    precision 83–84
    schedules, use of 73
    short sentences 49, 69, 134
    simplicity 58, 75, 82, 84, 134
    structure 70–74, 79, 81, 129, 132, 152, 157
    tone 21, 23, 71, 157
Plain Language Act, 1980 (USA) 46
Plain Language Act, possibility in South Africa 158
*Plain Language Guide, The* 81
Plain Language Institute 29, 158
Plain legal language, not previously a priority 9
Polish Society of Economic, Legal and Court Translators (TEPIS) 104–105
Precision 79, 82, 84
Presidential memorandum (USA) 49
Promotion of Administration of Justice Act (3 of 2000) 157

Questionnaire 42, 87, 94, 123, 126, 129–130, 132–133, 136

Roman Dutch Law 89, 93, 104

*Scribes Journal of Legal Writing, The* 51
Security and Exchange Commission (USA) 47
"Shall" 66–67
Skills Development Act 129
Sources on plain language
    general 163
    South African focus 169
South African Law Commission 87
South African Schools Act 1996 85
South African Translator's Institute (SATI) 92
Soweto uprising 9
Spoken language 21
State law advisers – drafting process 14–15, 83–84
Supreme Court Rules (USA) 48
Sweden, plain language in 30

Tax, language in legislation 40, 174
Technical Refinement Team 63, 65

Term creation 100–101
Terminology 13, 26, 69, 89–91, 92–94, 96,
    100–101, 103, 105–106, 109–110,
    112–114, 173
Translation (translating) 10, 20, 22, 34,
    21–22, 59, 78, 92, 97, 101
Transliteration 101–103, 106
*Trilingual Dictionary of Criminal Law,
    Criminal Procedure and Law of
    Evidence* 94

Unfair Terms in Consumer Contract
    Regulations 1994 38
Unification 109–110, 112, 114, 116, 118
United Kingdom, plain language in 29
United States of America, plain
    language in 29, 45
University of Pretoria 12–13, 15, 19, 45,
    123, 157, 175–176

Versions of plain language 38, 129–130
Veterans Benefits Administration (USA)
    46

Webpages on plain language
    general 169
    South African focus 169
WesBank 14, 86, 88, 175
World Bank of International Terms
    (WBIT) 38, 110, 173
World Encyclopaedia of International
    Terms 111
Written language 22, 59, 90, 114